Millennials

&

K-12 SCHOOLS

EDUCATIONAL STRATEGIES
FOR A NEW GENERATION

**Neil Howe &
William Strauss**

WITH REENA NADLER

Millennials

&

K-12 SCHOOLS

Howe, Neil and Strauss, William
Millenials & K–12 schools

ISBN: 0-9712606-5-6
ISBN-13: 978-0-9712606-5-8

Table of Contents

PART FOUR: GRADUATION AND BEYOND

Foreword

In my 35 years as an educator, I have observed k–12 schools from many different perspectives, as a teacher, PTA leader, community activist, and school-board leader. I have also had the opportunity to learn a great deal about generations while acting as a sounding board for the generational research of my husband, Bill Strauss, and his co-author Neil Howe. Over the years, I have offered Bill and Neil many practical, on-the-ground observations on the issues educators encounter in our day-to-day work. And I have observed firsthand how much the school landscape has changed as different generations of students passed through, new generations of teachers brought new sets of priorities, and parent constituencies shifted dramatically.

In my own Fairfax County, Virginia, district, some of the shifts have been dramatic. Today's students accept security measures in school buildings as the norm, from surveillance cameras to uniformed police officers to walking between classes with an assigned "hall buddy." They like group work and expect to encounter team projects in just about every class across the curriculum. Ambitious students are crowding every possible AP or IB class into their already-packed schedules. At the same time, parents are demanding data-driven decision making, transparency, and assessment. They request Blackboard programs that keep them constantly up to date about what their child is learning. In short, they support the call to leave "no child behind"—especially their *own* child. Younger teachers are flocking to professional learning communities, supporting teacher incentives, and embracing new technologies that promote a "just in time" model of teaching and productivity.

Understanding generations can give us the "big picture" perspective to make sense of these trends. That is what this book offers educators: fresh insight on

how we can best serve the new population of students, align our priorities with the new community of parents, and fulfill the mission of our schools in the decades to come.

Jane K. Strauss,
Member of the Fairfax County School Board

It is said that generals are always planning to win the last war, not the war they are now fighting. Likewise, it may be said that educators are always crusading to fix the problems of the last generation of students, not the generation they are now schooling.

Today's educators often advocate K–12 reforms that are designed to cope with a familiar, unchanging, and alarmist litany of youth problems—ranging from low test scores and civic disengagement to rising apathy and rampant personal risk taking. This makes sense only if you ignore generational change. Yes, most of these dire trends were important when today's educators (especially Baby Boomers and Generation Xers) were young. But in fact they no longer describe the behavioral or attitudinal direction of today's rising Millennial Generation.

Because generations are shaped by the distinct eras in which they are raised, each new youth generation is different from the last. Each arrives with its own new strengths and vulnerabilities. If today's educators pay no attention to such differences, their K–12 policy initiatives will miss their target. They will fail to harness new Millennial strengths (such as teamwork, longer time horizons, or closeness to parents). And they will fail to guard against new Millennial weaknesses (such as trouble handling risk and failure or excessive pressure to conform and achieve). Today's educators, in short, will be planning for the last war.

The arrival of Millennials is not the only generational shift underway. Older generations are maturing as well, in ways that are also having a major impact on K–12 schools.

As Gen Xers reach the cusp of midlife, they are replacing Boomers as the dominant generation of parents and teachers. Xer parents bring with them a

new focus on accountability, transparency, and choice. Xer teachers push flexibility and the bottom line. Boomers too are getting older. They are now ascending to senior positions as board members, superintendants, and nonprofit executives. As they replace the more process-minded Silent Generation who used to fill those posts, Boomers are drawing attention (as always) with their crusading, values-driven, and workaholic style of leadership.

Bill Strauss and I began studying American generations over twenty years ago. We identified (and labeled) the "Millennial Generation" in the late 1980s, when the oldest were still just entering elementary school. In *Generations*, published in 1991, we described how these children rode "a powerful crest of protective concern" in an adult world that was "rediscovering an affection and sense of responsibility for other people's children." When most youth assessments were downbeat, even grim, we forecast that as these new children passed through adolescence "substance abuse, crime, suicide, unwed pregnancy will all decline." We made similar predictions for teen employment and television viewing.

When these nonlinear predictions all came to pass, we were not surprised. There were good reasons for our predictions, rooted in how the Millennials were being raised, in how the lineup of older generations was shifting, and in the rhythms of history itself.

We wrote *Millennials and K–12 Schools* at the urging of many teachers, principals, administrators, and support personnel in public and private schools who, after having read our books or heard our lectures, agreed with us that Millennials are in fact arriving—and have asked us how their institutions can better serve them. An earlier version of this text appeared as a twin set of essays we published in *The School Administrator* (published by the American Association of School Administrators) in September of 2005. With this volume, we now offer an updated and much-expanded presentation.

In Part One of this book, we summarize the basic facts about today's new youth generation. We explain its location in history in relation to older generations. We introduce the seven core Millennial traits: special, sheltered, confident, team oriented, conventional, pressured, and achieving.

In Part Two, we explain how K–12 schools can best prepare and respond to each of these traits. We cover the entire gamut of policy areas, ranging from

curriculum, exams, counseling, college prep, No Child Left Behind (NCLB), tech prep, small schools, alignment to security, health, dropping out, counseling, fund raising, parents, voters, awards, and gender wars.

In Part Three, we look at how the aging of other generations is also transforming K–12 schools. Perhaps the biggest change is the advent of Gen-X parents (and voters). We also examine changes in the generations of teachers and school leaders. Nearly all of the teachers now retiring from the profession are Boomers; most of the new hires are themselves Millennials. Finally, we take a quick look at the post-Millennial 'Homeland' Generation, soon to arrive at a kindergarten near you.

By necessity, we can only cover so much ground here. For readers who wish to learn more, we recommend *Millennials Rising* (2000), which we published just as the much-celebrated high school "Class of 2000" was graduating from high school. We also recommend *Millennials Go to College* (2006) and *Millennials in the Workplace* (forthcoming).

If you would like to learn more about our historical method, would like to see what we've written about Millennials in earlier years, or would like to pursue your own research on generational topics, please see *Generations* (1991) and *The Fourth Turning* (1997). To see what we wrote about Gen Xers when they were collegians and young adults, please see *13th-Gen* (1993), which we published when today's 35-year olds were graduating from college.

Finally, let me express my great sorrow at not being able to byline this preface with my long-time co-author. Bill Strauss passed away in December of 2007. Over the last decade, Bill spent much of his time tutoring and working with talented Millennials, and everyone who knew him quickly understood how passionate he was about this generation's potential. Thousands of K–12 teachers in particular found his message inspiring. He believed that no matter how much we Boomers, as Old Aquarian leaders, may stir up trouble, this generation will be able to save America and build us up to a higher standard of greatness.

For this reason, we dedicate this book to Bill.

Neil Howe
September, 2008

Acknowledgments

The authors would like to thank a number of individuals for their contributions to this book. Most importantly, we would like to thank Reena Nadler, whose work as a contributing author has been invaluable. Without her incisive vision, writing skill, and tireless dedication, this book would not have been possible. We would also like to thank Jack Congdon, whose careful editing and data analysis have significantly enhanced this book; Rick Delano for his marketing acumen; Victoria Hays, for her careful attention to the countless details behind a project like this; and Jim Graham, whose cover design and layout truly pull the book together.

PART ONE

Meet the Millennials

"Meet the Millennials, and rejoice."

— ANNA QUINDLEN, *NEWSWEEK* (2000)

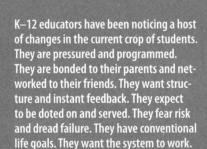

K–12 educators have been noticing a host of changes in the current crop of students. They are pressured and programmed. They are bonded to their parents and networked to their friends. They want structure and instant feedback. They expect to be doted on and served. They fear risk and dread failure. They have conventional life goals. They want the system to work.

Meet the Millennials.

Who are these new students? What makes them so different from the students who filled schools in the 1970s and 1980s? Here we explain how this rising Millennial generation of students is recasting the youth mood in America. We identify the misconceptions that abound about them, trace the social forces have shaped their childhood, and explain the resulting turnaround in key youth attitudes and trends.

1 | A New Generation

"There has been a faulty portrayal
of Millennials by the media—
television, films, news, blogs,
everything. These people are
not the self-entitled, coddled
slackers they're made out to be.
Misnomers and myths about
them are all over the place."

— ANN MACK, TREND SPOTTER AT JWT (2008)

To hear many educators tell it, their biggest problem these days is America's rising expectations of school performance.

The media keep repeating how the global economy will soon require nearly all young Americans to be fully prepared for postsecondary education. Legislators keep ratcheting up Standard of Learning and No Child Left Behind thresholds and dictating whole new teaching methods and subject areas. Parents are getting pushier than ever—demanding special attention, more options, and instant results. According to a recent MetLife poll, K–12 teachers say that "parents" have become their number one professional headache.

3

Yet there is another problem, less discussed but probably more serious: America's falling expectations of what the rising youth generation is capable of achieving.

Each month, new books and newspaper articles criticize today's young people for everything from poor grammar and short attention spans to flip flops and spaghetti straps. One recent book (by Mark Bauerlein) calls them *The Dumbest Generation*. Another (by Jean Twenge) calls them *Generation Me*. According to the editors of the *Wall Street Journal*, they are "Generation E, for Entitled." According to Hillary Clinton, "they think work is a four-letter word."

It is often assumed that that today's new batch of kids is fated by history to continue along the path blazed by young Boomers and then trampled by young Gen Xers. Toward more selfishness in dress and manners. Toward more splintering in life goals. Toward more profanity in the culture. Toward more risks with sex, drugs, and crime. Toward more apathy about politics. And toward less interest in academic excellence and credentialed achievement.

Some pundits—marketers especially—have dubbed today's young people "Generation Y," as though they are merely Generation X on steroids, South Park idiots beyond redemption, the ultimate price for America's post-1960s narcissism. A study recently published in the academic journal, *Social Policy Research*, finds American adults take a dim view of the younger generation. Among the findings:

* Only 16 percent of adult Americans agree that people under the age of thirty share most of their moral and ethical values.
* The three most frequently reported topics of youth news on the local stations are crime victimization, accidents involving young people, and violent juvenile crime, accounting for nearly half of all youth coverage.
* When asked to comment on recent unbiased news items about teenagers, adults consistently overlooked the positive data (that dominated the story) and focused instead on the few negative trends.

The data are clear—and reflect a profound disconnect between the good news about today's teens and the adult misperception of them. According to a recent national survey, barely one adult in three thinks that today's kids, once

grown, will make the
world a better place.

How depressing.
And how wrong.

How Millennials
are Different

Yes, there is a new
batch of youth com-
ing on stage—the
Millennial Genera-
tion, born since 1982,
whose leading-edge
members were the
celebrated high
school Class of
2000. But contrary
to expectations, this
generation is a trend
turner. Look closely
at youth indicators,
and you'll see that
the Millennials' atti-
tudes and behaviors

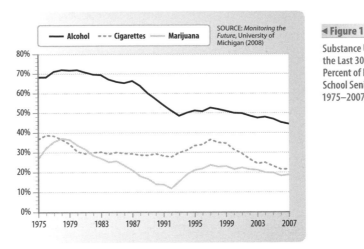

Substance Use in
the Last 30 Days,
Percent of High
School Seniors,
1975–2007

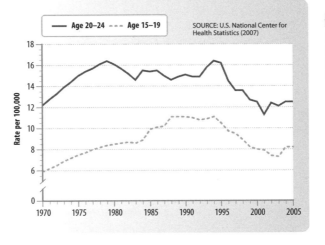

◄ Figure 2

Suicide Rates
for Youth, Aged
15–19 and 20–24,
1970 to 2005

represent a sharp break from Generation X, and are running exactly counter
to trends launched by the Boomers. Across the board, today's young people
are challenging the dominant and negative stereotype.

Are they pessimists? No. They're optimists. Nine in ten describe themselves
as "happy," "confident," and "positive." Teen suicide rates are trending downward
for the first time since World War II. A rapidly decreasing share of teenagers
worry about violence, sex, or drugs, and a rapidly increasing share say that
growing up is easier for them than it was for their parents.

Are they rule breakers? No. They're rule followers. Over the past fifteen years, rates of violent crime among teens have dropped by over 65 percent, rates of teen pregnancy and abortion by 40 percent, rates of high school sexual activity by 15 percent, and rates of alcohol and tobacco consumption are hitting all-time lows. As public attention to K–12 school shootings has risen, their actual incidence has fallen. Even including such shootings as Columbine, there have been fewer than half as many killings by students since 1998 (averaging fewer than 15 per year) as there were in the early 1990s (over 40 per year). According to "Youth Risk Behavior" surveys run by the Centers for Disease Control and Prevention, risk taking is down across the board for high school students—in everything from binge drinking to not buckling your seatbelt.

Are they self absorbed? No. From service learning to team grading to MySpace, they are gravitating toward group activity. Twenty years ago, "community service" was unheard of in most high schools. Today it is the norm,

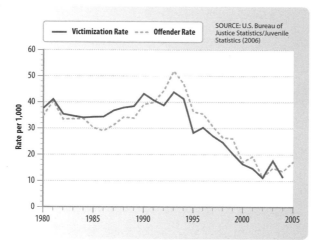

Figure 3 ▶

Serious Violent Crime, Rate of Offenders and Victims Aged 12–17, 1980 to 2005*

*2004 for Victims

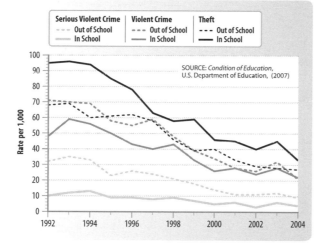

Figure 4 ▶

Theft & Crime Victims Age 12–18, in School and Out-of-School, Rate per 1,000

having more than tripled since 1984, according to the U.S. Department of Education. A 1999 Roper *National Youth Opinion* survey found that more teen-agers blamed "selfish-ness" than anything else when asked about "the major cause of problems in this country."

Are they distrust-ful? No. They accept authority. Most teens say they identify with their parents' values, and more than nine in ten say they "trust" and "feel close to" their par-ents. A recent survey found 82 percent of teens reporting "no problems" with any family member— versus just 48 per-cent who said that back in 1974, when parents and teens were far more likely to argue and oppose one another's basic values. Half say they trust government to do what's right all or most of the time—twice the share of older people answering the same question in the same poll. Large majorities of students favor tougher rules against misbehavior in the classroom and society at large.

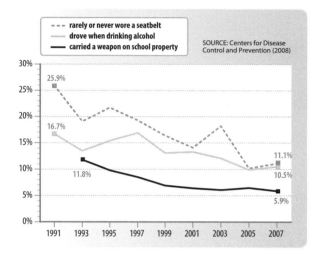

◀ Figure 5

Share of High School Students from 1991 to 2007 Who Report Having...

(Drinking and seatbelts, over last 30 days; weapon, over last 6 months)

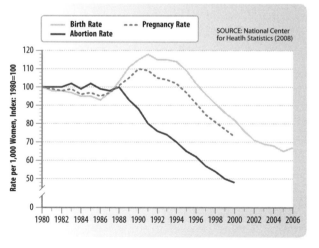

◀ Figure 6

Rates of Pregnancy, Abortion, and Birth for Girls Aged 15–17, Index: 1980 to 2006*

*2000 for Pregnancies and Abortions

Are they neglected? No. They're the most watched-over generation in memory. The typical day of a child, 'tween, or teen has become a nonstop

round of parents, relatives, teachers, coaches, babysitters, counselors, chaperones, minivans, surveillance cams, and curfews. Whether affluent or not, kids have become more closely managed. Since the mid-1980s, "unstructured activity" has been the most rapidly *declining* use of time among preteens.

Figure 7 ▶

Number of AP
Exams with Grade
of 3, 4, or 5, in all
U.S. Public Schools:
% Increase
Since 1997

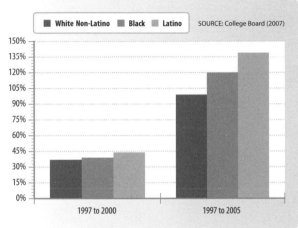

Are they stupid? No. Since the late 1980s, grade school aptitude test scores have been rising or (at least) flat across all subjects and all racial and ethnic groups. The number of high school students who take and pass an Advanced Placement (AP) test has more than doubled in the past ten years. Fully 70 percent of high school students today say they want a four-year college degree. A growing share are taking the SAT or ACT. Even so, the average score on these national tests is the highest in thirty years. Eight in ten teenagers say that it is "cool to be smart."

Are they another "lost" generation? No. A better word is "found." Born in an era when Americans showed a more positive attitude toward children, the Millennials are the product of a birthrate reversal. During the Gen-Xer childhood, planned parenting meant contraceptives; during the Millennial childhood, it has meant visits to the fertility clinic. In 1989, U.S. births exceeded four million for the first time since the early 1960s. And in 1998, the number of U.S. children surged past its previous peak in the early 1970s.

Not only do many people miss these positive youth trends, they also miss the new youth problems that have arisen as a result of these trends—problems that are very different from the ones Boomers and Gen Xers faced in their youth.

So pressured are Millennials to meet adult expectations that many fear taking creative risks. They know the stakes are high, and they perceive that the price of

any mistake, whether a wrong choice or a bad grade, is more consequential than it used to be. Teachers report that it is harder to get students to think outside the box. They also report that students who work so hard to pass tests and meet teacher expectations have a hard time understanding why plagiarism is wrong.

So team-oriented are Millennials that many would rather seek consensus and the approval of the group than assert a divisive or controversial opinion. Social bullying has become a rising problem among today's kids and teens as the importance of peer groups has increased. Social outsiders can feel greater pain and even be more likely to lash out.

So special do Millennials feel that many have trouble facing criticism, coping with failure, and sticking with any activity that may at first prove disappointing.

So trusting are Millennials of the institutions in their lives that they face particularly bitter disappointment when the system does not deliver success for everyone.

So sheltered are Millennials by their parents that many have trouble developing strong independent coping skills. Overly involved and intrusive parents have become a real hassle for many educators. Youth obesity is on the rise as kids spend more time in sedentary activities and less time playing independently out of doors.

Boomers started out as the objects of loosening child standards in an era of conformist adults. Millennials have started out as the objects of tightening child standards in an era of nonconformist adults. Educators who define today's students by their image of students past will miss the many new positive trends—and they will miss the chance to help this generation with the new set of challenges they face as they rise into adulthood.

Generational Location in History

Why is the widespread perception of "Generation Y" so off the mark? For the simple reason that the predictive assumption is wrong. Whatever the era they are living in, Americans habitually assume that the future will be a straight-line extension of the recent past. But that never occurs, either with societies or with generations. Every generation is uniquely shaped by its own location in history, and that formative influence has enduring effects.

Reflect for a moment on a few earlier examples. The unusually rule-abiding Silent Generation (born 1925–1942) were children during the crisis years of the Great Depression and World War II. They defined youth in the 1940s and 1950s, the so-called "golden age" of the comprehensive high school.

The more argumentative and values-obsessed Boom Generation (born 1943–1960) were children during an era of postwar complacency. They defined youth in the 1960s and 1970s, an era of social turmoil, youth anger, and steeply worsening educational outcomes.

The pragmatic and survivalist Generation X (born 1961–1981) were children during the Consciousness Revolution. They defined youth in the 1980s and 1990s, an individualistic era of market-driven free agency.

Likewise, the Millennial Generation has its own location in history.

Recall the last quarter century of American family life. The change came in 1982. The February 22, 1982 issue of *Time* Magazine offered a cover story about an array of thirtysomething Boomers choosing (finally) to become moms and dads. That same year, bright yellow "Baby on Board" signs began popping up in station wagon windows.

Around Christmas of 1983, adult America fell in love with Cabbage Patch Kids—a precious new doll, harvested pure from nature, so wrinkly and cuddly-cute that millions of Boomers wanted to take one home to love. Better yet, why not a genuine, live Millennial?

The era of the wanted child had begun.

In September 1982, the first Tylenol scare led to parental panic over trick-or-treating. Halloween suddenly found itself encased in hotlines, advisories, and statutes—a fate that would soon befall many other once-innocent child pastimes, from bicycle riding to BB guns.

A few months later came national hysteria over the sexual abuse of toddlers, leading to dozens of adult convictions after what skeptics will liken to Salem-style trials.

All the while, new books (*The Disappearance of Childhood, Children without Childhood, Our Endangered Children*) assailed the "anything goes" parental treatment of children since the mid-1960s. Those days were ending as the family, school, and neighborhood wagons began circling.

The era of the protected child had begun.

Through the early 1980s, the national rates for many behaviors damaging to children—divorce, abortion, violent crime, alcohol intake, and drug abuse—reached their postwar high water mark. The wellbeing of children began to dominate the national debate over most family issues: welfare, latchkey households, drugs, and pornography.

In 1983, the federal *Nation at Risk* report on education blasted grade school students as "a rising tide of mediocrity," prompting editorialists to implore teachers and adults to do better by America's next batch of kids.

In 1984, *Children of the Corn* and *Firestarter* failed at the box office. Hollywood was astonished, since these were merely the latest installments in a child-horror film genre that had been popular and profitable for nearly two decades, ever since *Rosemary's Baby* and *The Exorcist*. But parents were beginning to prefer a new kind of movie (*Baby Boom, Parenthood, Three Men and a Baby*) about adorable babies, wonderful tykes, and adults who improve their lives by looking after them.

The era of the worthy child had begun.

In 1990, the *Wall Street Journal* and *New York Times* had headlines—"The '60s Generation, Once High on Drugs, Warns Its Children" and "Do As I Say, Not As I Did"—that would have been unimaginable a decade earlier. Polls showed that Boomer parents did not want their own children to have the same freedom with drugs, alcohol, and sex that they once enjoyed.

By the early '90s, elementary school kids were in the spotlight. During the Gulf War Super Bowl of 1991, children marched onto the field at halftime amid abundant media coverage (unseen during the Vietnam War) of the children of dads serving abroad.

Between 1986 and '91, the number of periodicals offered to young children doubled. In tot-TV fare, *Barney and Friends* (featuring teamwork and what kids share in common) stole the limelight from *Sesame Street* (featuring individualism and what makes each kid unique).

During 1996, major-party nominees Dole and Clinton dueled for the presidency in a campaign full of talk about the middle school children of "soccer moms."

The next year, Millennials began to make an impression on the pop culture. Thanks to the Spice Girls, Hanson, and others, 1997 ushered in a whole new musical sound—happier, brighter, and more innocent.

The era of the perfected child had begun.

Through the late 1990s, the first wave of these much-watched children passed through high school, accompanied by enormous parental, educational, and media fascination. After the April 1999 Columbine tragedy was replayed again and again on the news, this adult absorption with Millennial safety, achievement, and morality reached a fever pitch.

The rising passions of adults crusading on behalf of kids helps explain why so little of the good news about Millennial behavior gets public attention. Quite simply, the good news is never good enough. The bad behavior has been declining, but the public tolerance of bad behavior has been declining even faster. Surveys indicate, as a result, that both parents and teachers have a stunningly higher perception of how their own kids are doing than of how kids generally are doing. When asked about their parenting skills, parents give themselves an A or B—but give all other parents a D or F.

So how are the positive youth trends evolving for the later-wave Millennials, born in the 1990s and early '00s? In many ways, these trends are intensifying, toward more protection, higher achievement, and declining risk. Yet there will be one important difference: The first half of the Millennial generation, born in the 1980s, have mostly Boomer parents while the second half, born in the '90s and early '00s, have mostly Gen-X parents.

A parental shift occurs about midway through every generation of youth. Generations tend to span about twenty birth years, with the first half born mostly to parents of the second prior generation and the second half born mostly to parents of the immediately prior generation. The older group of parents set the dominant parenting tone for each generation of youth. Recall how the World War II-winning G.I. Generation became the suburban parents of K–12 Boomer students in the mid-1950s. There they established a "father knows best" family order that set the stage for Boomers' Consciousness Revolution rebellion, leading to rising risk taking and falling achievement. The Silent Generation intensified this parenting style when they raised later cohorts

of K–12 Boomer students in the mid-1960s—and late-wave Boomers turned out even more rebellious and risk prone.

A similar shift is playing out today, but with youth behavior trending in the opposite direction. Gen-X parents are intensifying the emotionally close, protective parental style pioneered by Boomers—and late-wave Millennials will be even more trusting of parents, risk averse, and achievement oriented than their older early-wave peers.

By the time the last Millennials come of age, they could become the best-educated youths in American history and the best-behaved young adults in living memory. But they may also have a tendency toward copying, consensus, and conformity that educators will want to challenge. The new Millennial trends, both positive and negative, will require broad changes in educational strategy.

2 | Millennials by the Numbers

> "Millennials have the potential to be a great generation … [that will] rise to the occasion and show courage, character, determination, innovation, and vision in ways that really make the country a better place."
>
> — DAVE VERHAAGEN, IN *PARENTING THE MILLENNIAL GENERATION* (2006)

To demographers and economists, each new generation brings with it a new batch of numbers and trend lines. One good test of whether we can draw an accurate qualitative profile of a generation is whether this profile matches the numbers. Let's take a new look at Millennials by the numbers: their size, their diversity, the hours they play, the brands they buy, and the reasons they work.

The Baby Boomlet

The best-known single fact about the Millennial Generation is that it is large. Already, America has well over 90 million Millennials. By the time future immigrants join their U.S.-born peers, this generation will probably top 100

million members. In native births per birth year (expected to average 3.9 million), Millennials will greatly exceed Gen Xers, edge out Boomers, and tower over every earlier generation in America.

Since most Millennials born in the 1980s are the children of Baby Boomers, the media often refers to them as America's new "Baby Boomlet" or "Echo Boom" generation.

Figure 8 ▶

Total U.S. Births, in Millions, 1950 to 2007

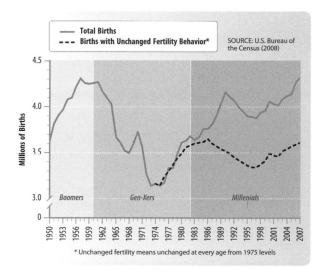

In two key ways, these terms are misleading. First, the 1990s-born Millennials—the larger half of the generation— are primarily the children of Gen Xers, not Boomers. Second, these terms imply that the large number of Millennials is mainly a matter of arithmetic, as though a "Baby Boomlet" mechanically had to issue from "Baby Boom" parents. In fact, the echo effect accounts for only a small part of the rise. For the most part, what gave rise to the large number of Millennials was the passionate desire of their parents to bear and raise more of them.

The larger than expected size of this generation is an extension of the early-'80s shift in adult attitudes toward children. The arrival of the first Gen Xers in the early '60s coincided with a sharp decline in the U.S. fertility rate and a society-wide aversion to children. And so it remained for the following twenty years, as small children seldom received positive media, while adults complained to pollsters about how family duties hindered their self discovery. Children became linked to new adjectives: unwanted, at risk, throwaway, homeless, latchkey.

All of this began to change with a surge in new births during the late 1970s and early '80s. Most experts at the time explained this as a delayed echo from the large number of Boomer women entering their prime child-bearing age—

and they predicted the echo would be short lived. They were in for a surprise. After leveling off at about 3.6 million from 1980 to 1983, the national birth rate did not drift back down. Instead, it rose—to 3.8 million in 1987, 4.0 million in 1989, and 4.2 million in 1990. Overall, Millennial births have been roughly 20 percent higher than if the fertility of women at each age had remained steady at mid-'70s rates.

What's important about this "baby boomlet" is how sustained it became and how it has reflected a resurgent adult desire to have kids. During the 1960s and '70s, the era of Gen-X babies, adults went to great efforts *not* to produce children, driving up the demand for contraceptive technologies and for sterilization and abortion clinics. During the Millennial baby era, by contrast, adults have gone to great efforts to conceive and adopt babies. Sterilization rates, which rose sharply in the 1960s and '70s, plateaued in the mid-'80s and have since fallen. The annual abortion rate, after ramping up during the Gen-X baby era, hit a peak in 1980 and declined over the next twenty-five years. Meanwhile, the share of all births declared to be "unwanted" by their mothers has also declined—with an especially sharp drop in unwantedness by African-American mothers.

Demographically, Millennials have two birth peaks with a shallow valley in between. The first (mainly Boomer-parented) 1990 peak of the Millennial birth bulge has been rippling up the school age ladder for some time now. Primary schools felt it in the late 1990s, middle schools just after 9/11, and now these teens are graduating from high schools. The second (mainly Gen-X-parented) 2000 peak is still pushing its way through elementary schools. These later-wave Millennials won't graduate from high school until 2018.

The final birth year of the Millennial Generation is yet to be determined. It may belong to those children who were born just after 9/11, or perhaps some other generational boundary will emerge. Time will tell. Over the past two centuries in America, generations have ranged in length from seventeen to twenty-four years, a span that suggests that the final Millennials will be those born sometime between 1999 and 2006. As we discuss in chapter 15, the next batch of children—we call them the Homeland Generation—will include children of Gen-X and Millennial parents. They will start enrolling in first grade no later than 2012.

Colors of the World

Millennials are the least white and most racially and ethnically diverse genera-tion in U.S. history. As of 2007, nonwhites and Latinos accounted for 41 per-cent of the population age twenty-five or under, nearly two-thirds larger than the share for Boomers, and more than double the share for today's seniors.

Millennials also have a much greater range of global diversity than Boomers did during their own school days. The issue of color can no longer be defined in clear black-white (or even black-white-Latino) terms. A class full of Millennial students, even when one looks just at American citizens, can include young women and men whose ancestors come from nearly every society on earth, including regions that were far less represented in 1960s schools.

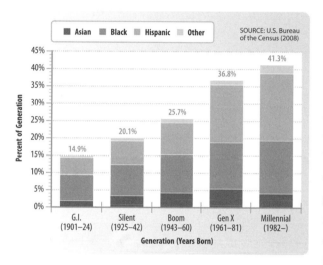

Figure 9 ▶

Non-White Race
and Hispanic
Ethnicity, by
Generation,
in 2007

To this point, Millennials are less often immigrants themselves than the children of immi-grants. In 2003, just fewer than 5 percent of Millennials were immigrants them-selves, versus 17 percent of Gen Xers and 12 percent of Boomers. Yet one Millennial in five has at least one immigrant parent, and one in ten has at least one non-citizen parent. Containing more second-generation immigrants than any earlier twenty-year cohort group in U.S. history, Millennials embody the "browning" of American civilization.

Thanks to the Cold War's end, satellite news, porous national borders, and the Internet, they are also becoming the world's first generation to grow up thinking of itself, from childhood forward, as global. For Millennials, therefore, ethnicity is more often a question of mixed identity than of racial polarization. A variety of ethnic beauty pageants were held in 2005 and 2006 crowning

young women as "Miss Liberia USA," "Miss Vietnam USA," and "Miss Ethiopia North America," among others.

Indeed, American (and Canadian) students mark the leading edge of a new worldwide generation. Since World War II, the leading edges of new European generations have arrived roughly five years or so after those in America. European youth still have more of a Gen-X than Millennial aspect, but some observers in Europe and Asia are describing the emergence of a Millennial-style shift among young teens. In Germany, these new kids have been called the *Null Zoff* ("no problem") generation—in Sweden, *Generation Ordning* ("ordered generation").

Millennials are the first American generation in which Latinos clearly out-number African Americans. With over half having at least one immigrant parent, many young Latinos face a future full of hard challenges: One-third live in poverty, in substandard housing, and without health insurance. The rate at which Latinos in grades 10 to 12 drop out of school each year (9 percent) is much higher than the rate for non-Latinos (5 percent). Yet many Latino pop icons provide a distinctly Millennial feel with upbeat lyrics, colorful clothes, and close family ties. With parents even more attached to "family values" than the white adult majority, the Latino youth culture is setting a distinctly Millennial tone—positive, team playing, and friendly—in schools and neighborhoods from Boston to San Diego.

Asian teens are also a rapidly growing presence. Propelled by cultures that honor filial duty and credentialed achievement, teens from Chinese and Indian families have won a reputation among Millennials as stellar academic achievers—especially in math, science, and engineering. In most U.S. high schools today, they are hugely over-represented in honors and AP classes and among students with the highest grade point averages (GPAs) and test scores.

Dating back to Emancipation, African Americans have been an outsized cultural contributor to generational currents. In recent decades, we have seen this in civil rights (Silent), black power (Boomers), and hip hop (Gen Xers). That contribution continues today. To be sure, many largely minority inner-city schools face some of the toughest challenges in education today, from dropout rates to substance abuse to poor test score achievement. Yet urban

nonwhite youths—especially African Americans—are in many respects bigger contributors to this generation's emerging positive persona than white youths. Ask yourself these questions: Which kids are more likely to be wearing uniforms? Urban nonwhites. Whose schools are moving fastest on back-to-basics drilling and achievement standards? Urban nonwhites. Whose neighborhoods are producing the swiftest percentage decline in youth murder, teen drug use, child poverty, teen pregnancy, and school violence—and the swiftest percentage rise in test scores? Urban nonwhites.

Duke University social scientists combine twenty-five key indicators of adolescent wellbeing (from child poverty to teen crime to drug use) into a "Youth and Child Well-Being Index." The index not only shows a dramatic upward thrust starting in 1994—just when Millennials began occupying adolescence—it also shows that the improvement for Latino and African-American minorities has been considerably steeper than for the white majority.

Regionally, the (mostly minority) urban areas have shown the steepest gains. The suburbs are in the middle. The (mostly white) rural areas have shown the slowest gains, with the least decline—and in certain areas a continued rise—in many negative indicators, especially substance abuse.

Busy Around the Clock

Millennial teens may be America's busiest people.

Long gone are the old days of Boomer kids being shooed outside to invent their own games—or of Gen-X kids being left "home alone" with a "self-care" guide. The new reality is structure, planning, and supervision, from kindergarten through college and beyond.

From 1991 to 1998, according to University of Michigan researchers, eighth and tenth graders showed sharp reductions in the share of those who engage "every day" or "at least once a week" in such open-ended youth activities as going to movies, cruising in cars and motorcycles, or walking around shopping malls. Vast majorities of high school seniors say they are more looked after and have less free time than their older brothers and sisters at the same age. During the 1990s, the sale of student day planners soared from one million to fifty million. As 10-year old Stephanie Mazzamaro told *Time* magazine: "I don't have time to be a kid."

Researchers at the University of Michigan have compared weekly time diaries filled out by parents of preschool and elementary school kids age three to twelve in two different years, 1981 and 1997. The first group was all Gen X and the second group was all Millennial. What they found was stunning: a 37 percent decline in the amount of "unstructured" free time enjoyed by kids, from 52 to 33 hours per week.

Much of the extra time has been taken up by school, the single most expanded child activity. More kids age four and five (known in earlier generations as "preschoolers" are now in school. More grade schools have early morning classes, afterschool programs, and "extra learning opportunity" programs. More students are attending summer school, which is now mandatory in many districts for kids who score low on tests and sought-after by kids who want extra credits for the next year.

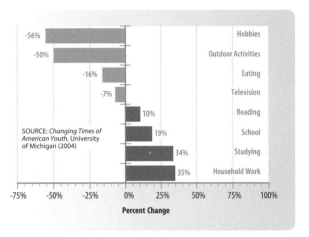

◄ Figure 10

Weekly Hours of Children Aged 6–17, by Activity Percent Change, from 1981 to 2003

The bottom line is this: Today's rising generation is busy—and often not in ways that today's adults can recall from their own youth. Millennial children are less likely to spend time lying on their backs imagining stories as the clouds roll by and more likely to spend time learning how to excel at standardized tests. They are less likely to play self-invented games with made-up rules, ending when they feel like it, and more likely to play on select teams with adult referees, professionalized rules, and published standings.

Teens Purchasing

Thus far, there has been much commercial interest in Millennials—how to make them watch an ad, how to make them buy, how to use them to make their parents buy. This is in part because people of many age brackets have been spending

more on children and teenagers in recent years—but also because teen marketers suddenly began to realize that generations matter. In the early 1990s, marketers awoke to the realization that they had never fully targeted Generation X, and were determined not to let this mistake recur with the next batch of kids.

There's no question that, today, a lot more cash is being spent on young people than ever before, as anyone who has recently visited a typical teen bedroom can attest. The first wave of this generation has grown up during an era of surging prosperity—from the early 1980s through the year 2000—when there was only one mild recession and the Dow Jones Index rose almost every year. Purchases by and for children age four to twelve tripled over the 1990s, and teens hit their stride at the decade's end.

In recent years, however, economic shocks, parental worries, high youth unemployment, and growing indebtedness among college-bound teens seem to be dampening the spending fire. One youth marketing firm finds that the purchasing volume flowing through the hands of Americans age twelve to nineteen shot up from $153 billion in 1999 to $172 billion in 2001—but since then has been zigzagging along a basically flat trajectory. In 2007, six years later, it had risen to only $179 billion. Considering population growth and inflation, this translates into an 11 percent *decline* in real (inflation-adjusted) spending per teen. By most estimates, the figure for 2008 will indicate an even steeper decline.

Such figures must be interpreted with care. It is increasingly hard to tell where a kid's own spending stops and where spending on his or her behalf begins. In recent years, people in every age bracket have been spending more on children and teenagers—youths themselves, parents on their own kids, and grandparents and other non-parents on young friends and relatives. Major companies keep adding new product lines just for Millennials, from Aquafresh for Kids, L'Oreal Kids, and Ozark Spring Water for Kids to Colgate SpongeBob SquarePants, TicTalk cell phones, and Sports Illustrated for Kids (with a special website, *www.sikids.com*). A new fashion trend has appeared in branded clothes lines just for kids, such as Gap Kids, Eddie Bauer Kids, and now even Sheen Kidz and Kidtoure t-shirts.

To be sure, most of this kid brand splurging is highly skewed toward the affluent. The distribution of kid and teen consumption directly reflects the

growing spread in the overall distribution of household income. Even the afflu-ent, moreover, have been hit by the recent economic downturn. High-end fashion-related purchases are down by an estimated 20 percent in 2008 alone. Nonetheless, surveys indicate that most Americans remain far more worried about too much youth consumption than too little. No one can fairly say these kids are collectively neglected. Rightly or wrongly, adults are favoring this new generation by steering more money toward its wants, and by identifying its wants with their own.

If the Millennial child spending boom has been fueled entirely by older people and not by their own (earned) income, where exactly does this money come from and how does it get spent? In fact, most of the increase comes from parental money. And, of this increase, most comes not in the form of regular allowances but rather through direct ad hoc payments from parent to child, often for specific purchases on which parent and child confer.

Since such payments are neither child spending nor parent spending, these consensual or joint transactions—which one in three teens says constitutes his or her biggest source of income—resist the categories favored by many market-ing experts. It works like this: Kids and teens ask parents for money to buy something, they together discuss whether it's a worthwhile purchase, the par-ents hand out the money, and the teens go to the store (or online) to make the purchase. Officials at the Center for a New American Dream have noted a new "nag factor" driving many youth purchases, with ten percent of 12- and 13-year olds saying they ask their parents more than fifty times for products they've seen advertised.

While parents are often paying in full for major teen purchases that in times past were more financed by youth work and savings, they also appear to be influencing lesser teen purchases through rules, advice, and earmarked cash. At the same time, teens are influencing parental purchase decisions on big-ticket items like cars, houses, and vacations (by voicing their opinion), and on small-ticket items like groceries and takeout food (by saving their parents time).

Thus has emerged the era of the parent-child "copurchase."

Twenty years ago, the big new trend in youth marketing was the independent child purchase. Today, the new trend is the child purchasing only after

receiving the parent's approval, alias the copurchase. The corollary of this is the "cotarget," where marketers treat the child and parent as influencers of each other's purchases, from a teen's school clothes to a mom's new car. To close the sale, you have to market to both parties.

This generation is not only transforming how young people buy products, it's changing the kinds of products they want to buy. Niche markets are foundering. Big brands are back. Aided by new technologies, from Web chat to cell phones, Millennials pay keen attention to what's happening at the gravitational center of their peer group, whether online at one of the new multiuser game sites, or in person at Target and Wal-Mart (both of which enjoyed post-9/11 boosts in teen buying). Mass fads, big brands, group focus, and a lower-profile commercial style are ready for a comeback. Meanwhile, "the edge" has peaked—along with weak product loyalties, hypercommercialism, and the focus on risk and self.

Mass marketers have taken full note of this. Calvin Klein and Abercrombie & Fitch, faced with softening demand for their labels, have recently retooled, replacing the ultra-edgy "in your face" approach that worked so well in the 1990s with a friendlier attitude clearly aimed at Millennials. Pepsi has also traded in edgy slogans and celebrity spots for community-oriented themes. Surveys show that television ads (and celebrity endorsements) are weakening as youth influencers, while peers and parents are rising in importance. If the economy continues to falter, Millennials will no doubt rally around low-priced versions of smart, upbeat, and family-friendly big brands. It's inconceivable that they would respond, as Gen-X youth did during the early '90s recession, with torn-flannel grunge, heroin chic, and a new wave of body piercings.

Whatever you're selling, from cars to soap to college, the way to connect with Millennials is to brand your image, target the mainstream, wrap yourself around positive youth values, and make room for the family in your message.

Organization Kids

During their 'tween and teen years, the experience of working for money outside the home has not been as common for Millennials as it was for previous generations—another measure of the extra sheltering and structure in their lives.

From one generation to the next, shifting parental and youth attitudes have played key roles in pushing teen employment up or down. For Boomer teens, the "right" to work was a newly won youth freedom. Then Gen Xers came along and pushed teen workloads higher. Allowing for the ups and downs of recessions, summer and afterschool teen work grew strongly and almost continuously from the mid-1960s to the early 1980s, and remained high for the rest of the 1980s.

In the Millennial youth era, by contrast, teen employment has trended downward. Amazingly, it hardly grew at all during the 1990s, despite a steadily accelerating economy that, through the year 2000, desperately wanted young workers and was willing to pay plenty for them. Then came another recession and 9/11. Teen employment plunged and has not recovered since. By 2005, the share of employed teens age sixteen to nineteen had fallen all the way to 36 percent (the lowest since records were first kept in 1948). It is plunging even further in 2008.

What accounts for the ebbing popularity of paid work for teenagers? One reason, accounting for about half of the decline, according to the U.S. Department of Labor, is that teens are spending more time in grade school (longer days and more summer school). Another reason is that attitudes have changed. During the '90s, educators, parents, and teens themselves began to have second thoughts about whether too many teens were wrapping tacos when they ought to be wrestling with math. When the bottom line is getting into a good college, time spent on select soccer, community service, or SAT prep courses seems more valuable, long term, than time spent solely on making money. As a result, many of the service jobs Gen-X teens once held are now held, not by Millennial teens, but by older Gen-X immigrants.

By the time Millennials become adults, this aversion to paid work apparently disappears. Adjusted for the business cycle, the employment rate of youths age twenty to twenty-four has been basically flat over the past twenty-five years, with no downward trend after 2000. Among college students, employment was actually higher in 2003 (a very weak year for the economy) than it was in 1979. This is a measure of the extra cost of college today—and of the pressure today's collegians feel to make ends meet.

Millennials have been entering the full-time workforce with high school degrees since 2000 and with four-year college degrees since 2004. Already, businesses are beginning to take stock of the opportunities and challenges this generation presents. On the plus side, employers report that they excel in group work, crave approval, are very teachable, like to plan their futures, and take a genuine interest in the overall purpose of the organization. On the negative side, employers report that they require a lot of oversight, avoid creative risks, are overly attached to their parents and families, and are unfamiliar with the bottom-line demands of paid employment. Some complain that today's young workers lack the "soft skills" (punctuality, politeness, proper dress, and so on) that earlier generations learned on the job at an earlier age. Others suggest, more constructively, that high schools and colleges make "workplace training" a required course for the entire student body.

3 | Grading the Millennials

"These teenagers seem to
be getting smarter and
smarter every year."

— ALEX TREBEK, TV HOST OF *JEOPARDY!* (2008)

Forty years ago, many a Boomer had big plans. So does many a Millennial today—but that's where the similarity ends.

As Boomers moved through school, from first wave to last—from the first "free speech" movement in 1964 to the widespread adoption of pass-fail systems in the late 1970s—youth expressed a growing resistance to being graded or ranked or categorized by the "system" for their achievements. Boomers preferred to be judged by who they were on the inside. Gradually, older Americans gave in to this new youth "counterculture" and grades and exams were deemphasized.

As Millennials have moved through school, youth have been pushing in the opposite direction. Students are worrying more about their grades, training

harder for achievement tests, and often even begging teachers to "evaluate" them before the score is due. Millennials prefer to be judged by what they do on the outside. As happened with Boomers, adults are accommodating the youth trend, this time by handing out a widening torrent of grades, stars, trophies, buttons, ribbons, and weekly online interim reports—so that even one-week summer camps feature endless rankings and prizes.

After graduating from high school, and especially in college, young Boomers made their biggest mark in the arts and humanities. As young professionals, they became precocious leaders in the media, teaching, advertising, religion—anything having to do with the creative rearrangement of values and symbols. Millennial youth show the opposite bent. Surveys reveal that they like math and science courses best, and the traditional humanities least. They like to spend free time in shared activities with friends instead of doing imaginative tasks on their own.

Their collective ambitions have a rationalist core. According to the LifeCourse *Class of 2000 Survey*, Millennial teens have a great deal of confidence in their generation's lifelong ability to improve technology (97 percent), race relations (77 percent), and the economy (55 percent)—all public and benchmarkable spheres of social life—but far less confidence in their prospects for improving more subjective areas such as the arts (31 percent), family life (20 percent), and religion (14 percent). Other surveys reveal teens as more likely than adults to value friendships, but less likely than adults to value the ability to communicate feelings.

Trends in academic achievement broadly reflect these generational shifts over time. When Boomers were in school, most achievement test scores showed a decline at every age as each passing Boomer cohort reached that age. Since Millennials have been in school, by contrast, most of the news on achievement has been positive.

Is the positive news justified? Yes, by and large. After weighing all of the evidence—and some of the evidence is not reassuring—one still must conclude that Millennials overall show substantial academic progress. All of the sweat and tears expended in recent years by voters, parents, schools, and students

Grading Earlier Generations

Some generations have a reputation for doing very well in school, and others do not. Each of today's living generations has acquired a distinct track record of academic achievement. Consider each in turn.

The **G.I. Generation** (born 1901 to 1924) achieved academic gains unmatched by any other generation in U.S. history. Civic achievers even as boy-scout and girl-scout youths, G.I.s thrived in school during a "progressive" era that featured huge investments in education and child protection legislation, including child labor laws. From first birth cohort to last, they pushed up average years of schooling from eight to eleven and the share of children graduating from high school from 15 percent to 50 percent. Benefitting from the G.I. Bill as young adults after World War II, they became the first generation to see a significant share of its middleclass receive postsecondary degrees.

The **Silent Generation** (born 1925 to 1942) maintained the high achieving reputation they inherited from late-wave G.I.s. The Silent stayed out of trouble, worried about their grades and "permanent records," and were the first students to rely on standardized tests (like the SAT) to advance to postsecondary education. A sharply increased share of this generation chose "professional" careers. According to surveys in the 1950s, the public believed that schools worked fine and that most teenagers were very smart. High school educators, believing they now knew what worked (the "comprehensive high school"), began increasing the size and scale of their schools to accommodate the large approaching baby boom.

The **Boom Generation** (born 1943 to 1960) pushed nearly every measure of academic achievement in a negative direction. At first, benefitting from reformed curricula and gleaming new facilities funded by the post-Sputnik National Defense Education Act, Boomers were hailed as the brightest kids ever. Then things fell apart. After peaking in 1963 (for the 1946 birth cohort), SAT scores fell for seventeen straight years until 1980. Exams in earlier grades reveal a similar decline. The achievement slide was probably linked to an alarming, simultaneous surge in dysfunctional behavior. From first birth cohort to last, Boomers triggered (at every age they passed through) a steady increase in alcohol consumption, drug abuse, unmarried teen pregnancy, suicide, self-inflicted accidents, and violent crime.

Generation X (born 1961 to 1981), ended the Boomer achievement decline, but maintained achievement levels that contemporary observers considered low and disappointing. Test scores such as the SAT and the *National Assessment of Educational Progress* (NAEP) didn't budge through the 1980s and only began rising again with late-wave Xers in the mid-1990s. First-wave Xers, born in the 1960s, are actually less likely than Boomers to have completed a college degree. Beginning with *A Nation at Risk* in 1983, national reports issued during the Xer teen era reached unremittingly negative conclusions about youth—that they don't read, don't study, don't vote, and don't care. Having survived a hurried childhood of divorce and open classrooms, many Gen Xers got around their poor start by proving themselves in the marketplace, turning to a self-help media and online courses, or going back to earn GEDs and postsecondary credentials later in life.

The **Millennial Generation** (born 1982–?) shows many signs of steady improvement—though the progress is not uniform and much of the story remains to be told. National college entrance exams (the ACT and SAT) show impressive gains combined with large increases in participation. The NAEP show large gains in some subjects (math and science) and modest or no gains in others (reading). In no subject are Millennials falling behind. A record share of high school graduates are entering college and intend to get their degrees before they start their careers. Meanwhile, the participation rate in Advanced Placement exams is soaring and the dazzling quality of today's extracurricular achievement (science fairs, tech contests, live and digital entertainment) simply speaks for itself.

have not gone to waste. If generations received grades, this one would surely deserve an improved mark.

Let's look first at scores from the two large college entrance exams. Since the early 1990s, SAT scores have risen dramatically, thanks initially to late-wave Gen Xers and later, even more decisively, to Millennials. After 2005, though the average SAT score unexpectedly fell (probably due to major changes in the exam, since the average ACT score continued to rise that year,) it still exceeded the score for every earlier year between 1974 and 2000. In the math component, recent scores are higher than at any time since the late 1960s. The ACT shows a similar growth trend. In 2008, the average ACT composite score was higher than in any year before 2006 and the ACT math score remained at a record high.

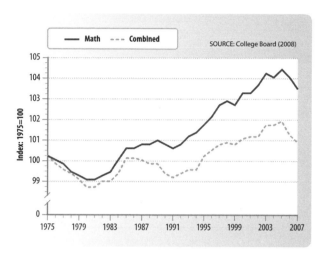

Figure 11 ▶

SAT Scores of College-Bound Seniors, 1975–2007 (1975=100)

These scores are rising, moreover, even as a much larger share of high school juniors and seniors are taking the exams than took it back in the early 1970s, in part because many states and districts are now requiring all students to take the exams. The share of high school graduates taking the SAT has grown from under one-third in the mid-1970s to nearly one-half (46 percent) in 2007. For the ACT, the growth in the test-taking share has been even more dramatic. The additional test takers include millions of poor and nonwhite youths, and the offspring of recent immigrants, who, back in the '60s and '70s, never would have tested at all. Remarkably, the share of nonwhites and Latinos taking the SAT has risen from 11 percent in 1973 to 39 percent in 2007. Had the exams been more accessible to minorities thirty years ago, the climb in the average score would likely have been even more dramatic.

Perhaps the most comprehensive benchmark for assessing overall student achievement is the National Assessment of Educational Progress (NAEP), the so-called "Nation's Report Card." According to the NAEP, the achievement of today's K–12 students is at the highest level ever in many subjects and has declined in none.

Math scores today are higher at every age than in any previous decade since the 1970s. Reading scores have either risen or remained steady at every age, and today they are higher at age nine than ever before. In grades four and eight, students have shown continual improvement in reading, history, geography, civics, and science. The rising NAEP trend is lifting all minority groups. The score gaps between white, black, and Latino students have been gradually shrinking over time.

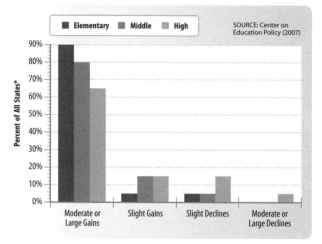

◄ Figure 12

Change in State *Math* Exam Scores Since 2002: for All K–12 Students

*Excluding those states (around 10 for most grade levels) having inadequate data

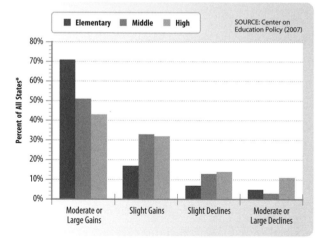

◄ Figure 13

Change in State *Reading* Exam Scores Since 2002: for All K–12 Students

*Excluding those states (around 10 for most grade levels) having inadequate data

State proficiency tests, which unlike the NAEP are tightly aligned to classroom curricula, show an even more dramatic improvement. According to a recent study by the Center on Education Policy, the vast majority of states

have shown moderate to large gains since 2002 in the number of students who are proficient in both reading and math. Across all grade levels, the number of states with moderate to large gains in percentages deemed proficient far outnumbered those with slight gains. Students have generally shown greater improvement in younger than in older grades, indicating a rising achievement trend by birth cohort.

The Trends in International Math and Science Study (TIMSS) also reports steady or rising achievement since 1995 in math and science. Eighth graders have moved from below to above the international average, and for first time in 2003, American students outscored Russians (whose world class reputation for math and science prowess once intimidated young Boomers). In the TIMSS, once again, minority students are making the biggest gains over time. Another international assessment, Progress in International Reading Literacy Study (PIRLS), tests fourth graders for their reading skills. In the most recent 2006 PIRLS exam, U.S. students ranked well above average.

Notwithstanding their good showing in the PIRLS, most of the indicators confirm that Millennials are making more progress in math than in verbal achievement. This may, in part, reflect a deficiency in the assessment exams, which test for neither new habits of reading and writing nor for the new realities of the digital age. From Web browsing to word processing to desktop publishing, today's students are adding new layers to the verbal skill sets that were taught to Boomers and Gen Xers at the same age. To date, the national assessments have had difficulty measuring these new skills—in particular, the SAT writing exam, which requires students to write a twenty-five minute essay in longhand, a task few of them ever have to do at home (or will have to do in the workplace).

Regardless of one's interpretation of test results, a solid consensus exists among K–12 educators that there is much room for improvement. High school dropout rates, while recently falling, remain distressingly high (especially for minorities). Among students who graduate from high school with good grades, a large share remain academically underprepared. Employers regularly complain that a high school degree does not qualify a young worker to advance beyond an entry level job, and well over half of all college instructors say they

spend at least part of their time teaching material that should have been taught by twelfth grade. Yet most of the public alarm over these shortcomings is driven by rising expectations about what the educational system should deliver to Millennials, not by objective evidence that it worked any better for earlier generations of youth.

Whatever the K–12 system's shortcomings, no one can blame them on Millennials, whose desire to achieve and succeed within the system exceeds that of any other youth generation in living memory. This desire is reflected in the unprecedented and still-rising share of high school students who aspire to go to four-year colleges, who take Advanced Placement courses and exams, and who sign up for academic summer camps and nonremedial summer school. Participation rates for the SAT and ACT are at record levels. According to the Department of Education's 2007 *Condition of Education* report, a rising share of high school graduates have completed advanced math, science, and language courses, and the share of tenth graders who spend more than ten hours per week on homework has climbed from 7 percent to 37 percent. Cynicism about school is passé. The 2005–06 Horatio Alger survey shows that 79 percent of high school students feel motivated or inspired to work hard. According to the 2005 *High School Survey of Student Engagement*, two-thirds say they take pride in their school work and place a high value on learning.

Many Millennials (urban minority teens, especially) feel that a major problem with the system is that it doesn't ask enough from them. The Horatio Alger survey found that 79 percent of high school students "feel strongly" that they would respond to higher academic standards by working harder. According to the National Governors Association, two-thirds say they would work harder if high school offered more demanding and interesting courses. A decisive majority supports standardized testing. Public Agenda has found that 80 percent of students would support higher academic standards even if it meant required summer school for those who fell short.

On the whole, Millennial dropouts reveal a similar attitude. In a recent survey of high school dropouts age sixteen to twenty-five, two-thirds say they would have worked harder if more had been demanded of them academically. Nearly all express remorse for not completing their degree, and most say it was

a mistake for the schools to let them "slip by." The remarkable success of "early college"—a rapidly expanding program in many states that takes high school student at risk of dropping out and enrolls them in college courses—shows how positively Millennials respond to high standards and to high expectations.

Millennials keep striving for achievement even when engaged in entirely optional activities outside the formal school curriculum. In middle and high schools, the quality and professionalism of extracurricular (what some call "cocurricular") programs are rising rapidly, from student governments to theater productions to specialized sports programs. Unprecedented numbers of students are bringing their organizing and high-tech skills to community service, sometimes even replacing adult professionals. Those who expect to win competitions for spelling, science, or debating must excel at a level unimaginable in prior decades. For earlier generations, much of what young people did outside of school was said to be "unstructured" and "informal." We no longer use such words to describe the intensity and specialization with which Millennials approach most of the activities in their lives.

DeWitt Clinton, an inner-city high school in the Bronx, looks like many other such schools in the Millennial era—crowded, ringed with metal detectors, and teeming with busy teens. DeWitt Clinton also enables over half of its incoming freshmen to go on to college and has been repeatedly voted one of the most improved schools in the nation. Homework is due in every class every day. Grades are based only on results, not aptitude or effort. The buildings bustle with high-octane extracurricular activities. The school's mission statement begins: "We believe that high expectations plus high standards equals high achievement." By this standard, Millennials are indeed achieving more—both in school and out—than other recent generations of youth.

4 | Seven Core Traits

"With their emphasis on teamwork, achievement, modesty, and respect for authority, today's high school graduates bear little resemblance to their more nihilistic Gen-X siblings and even less to their self-indulgent Baby Boomer parents."

— *MILWAUKEE JOURNAL SENTINEL* (2005)

Every generation contains all kinds of people. But each generation has a persona, with core traits. Not all members of that generation will share those traits, and many will personally resist those traits, but—like it or not—those core traits will substantially define the world inhabited by every member of a generation.

The following are the seven core traits of the Millennial Generation.

* **Special.** From precious-baby movies of the mid-1980s to the media glare surrounding the high school Class of 2000, older generations have inculcated in Millennials the sense that they are, collectively, vital to the nation and to their parents' sense of purpose.

35

* **Sheltered.** From the surge in child-safety rules and devices to the post-Columbine lockdown of public schools to the hotel-style security of today's college dorm rooms, Millennials have been the focus of the most sweeping youth-protection movement in American history.

* **Confident.** With high levels of trust and optimism—and a newly felt connection to parents and future—Millennials are equating good news for themselves with good news for their country.

* **Team Oriented.** From *Barney* and team sports to collaborative learning and community service, Millennials have developed strong team instincts and tight peer bonds.

* **Conventional.** Taking pride in their improving behavior and comfortable with their parents' values, Millennials provide a modern twist to the traditional belief that social rules and standards can make life easier.

* **Pressured.** Pushed to study hard, avoid personal risks, and take full advantage of the collective opportunities adults are offering them, Millennials feel a "trophy kid" pressure to excel.

* **Achieving.** As accountability and higher school standards have risen to the top of America's political agenda, Millennials have become a generation focused on achievement—and are on track to becoming the smartest, best-educated young adults in U.S. history.

PART TWO

Millennials in K-12 Schools

"The current generation of high school and college students is different from previous generations…. If you understand more about this generation and how they tick, you'll be better equipped to create a plan that will help you guide your students to success."

— MAKINGITCOUNT.COM, TRAINING AND COUNSELING DIVISION OF MONSTER (2007)

What should K–12 schools do to cope with the new Millennial students—and to prepare for the waves of the even more Millennial-style classes to come? How should the mission, organization, curriculum, recreation, discipline, and classroom experience of schools be retooled? Where should new money be spent? In this era of parent-child copurchasing, these are questions with two sets of answers—one set involving the students themselves, and the other involving older generations of parents and teachers.

In the next set of chapters, we address the student side. Here, the seven core Millennial traits hold the key. We explore the impact of each trait on K–12 school systems and discuss what this means for the superintendants, board members, principles, administrators, and teachers who work in them daily.

5 | Special

"They were raised by doting
parents who told them they are
special, played in little leagues
with no winners or losers, or all
winners. They are laden with
trophies just for participating."

— CBS *60 MINUTES* REPORT,
"THE MILLENNIALS ARE COMING" (2007)

Since birth, older generations have instilled in Millennials the sense that they
are the personal focus of adult inspiration and are collectively vital to the
nation. From kindergarten through college and beyond, parents are keeping
a closer watch over their children, often hovering over every aspect of their
lives. Alissa Quart calls them "Hothouse Kids" in a book by that title. A 2006
Newsweek survey shows that over two-thirds of parents of Millennials (especially the younger Gen-X parents) say they spend or have spent more time with
their children than their own parents spent with them. A similar share say they
talk with their children more.

Unlike older generations at the same age, Millennials have grown up watch-
ing adults (from supermoms to stay-at-home dads) define their life purpose

around their children. They have seen the media use images of children to portray life's deepest purpose—images so prevalent that now even AARP features cheerful kids in ads. They have heard politicians compete with each other to be seen as the most passionate about the welfare of children.

Meanwhile, as Millennials have aged through the K–12 school system, the glare of the media has followed them at every step—hitting elementary schools in the early 1990s, middle schools (with their "soccer moms") in the middle Clinton years, high schools during the late Clinton years, and finally college during the Bush years. Ever since the fall of 2000, when the oldest Millennials began graduating and the network news staged loud fanfare about the "High School Class of 2000," schools have become an all-Millennial media hot zone. Through steady news features about every grade level and through sweeping laws like No Child Left Behind, America has concentrated its attention on improving the quality of K–12 education for each of these very special children.

As Millennials absorb the parental message that they dominate America's agenda, they come easily to believe that their problems are the nation's problems. Ask Millennials about their preferred choice of community service, and most often they will tell you it's helping other people their own age, either at home or abroad.

When asked which groups will be most likely to help America toward a better future, teens rank "young people" second, behind only "scientists." When asked whose generation can have the greatest impact on what the global environment will become twenty-five years from now, 86 percent say their own, and only 9 percent say their parents'. When asked the same question, their parents mostly agreed, with 71 percent saying their children's generation will have the most impact.

The tightening bond between parent and child is raising new challenges for today's teachers, from frequent phone calls and visits by parents to new technologies allowing constant parental surveillance of classroom work. "When you teach now, you don't just get the child," explained one teacher. "You get the whole package—the mom, dad, sibling and even the grandparents." As parents become more involved in their children's education, new schools are

being designed as centers of public activity, with central gathering spaces available to afterschool groups and adults.

Putting *Special* to Use

❋ **Leverage individual goodwill among parents and families. Get "helicopter parents" on your side.**

According to recent MetLife surveys, K–12 teachers say that *parents* are now the number one on-the-job challenge—and also the challenge for which they received the least training. When faced with angry or meddling parents, teachers' first instinct is often to pull rank: Get out of the way, I am the professional. Fifteen or twenty years ago, that might have worked. But no longer. Today's moms and dads have raised their kids on William and Martha Sears' "attachment parenting." They cannot be too close to their kids, they want to be involved in every major decision, and (especially the younger Gen-X parents) they distrust big institutions. Straight-arming the parent after a problem arises will only trigger hostility and resentment—or even, in today's "choice" environment, parental efforts to put their child in another school.

With Millennials, schools and teachers must try a different strategy: Get parents to be your collaborators. Make an extra effort to establish personal relationships with parents at the beginning of the year. Harness and channel their energy. Have them read (or even sign) "covenants" spelling out how they can best help their child's learning and why that help is important. Schools should learn from the way colleges now carefully cater to parents, with two-day orientations and special college-parent partnership contracts, or the way the military has overhauled its recruiting message to stress a similar partnership theme ("You made them strong. We'll make them Army Strong"). Everyone who wants to reach children and teens now comarkets earnestly to their parents. K–12 schools need to do the same.

❋ **Prepare for youth who feel personally and generationally entitled, and use that self-esteem to fuel self-motivation.**

Some older people will regard a rising generation that knows it is special as poised and confident—and others will regard it as entitled, coddled, or

even "narcissistic." Older generations, who grew up in an era when youth were less fussed-over, often worry that young people who have experienced so little risk, criticism, disappointment, or adversity may have trouble assuming responsibility and motivating themselves to excel. The message that worked best with Gen-X students was: Do it right, because if you don't, no one else is going to help you. Clearly that message will no longer be effective with Millennials. So how can schools ready this special generation for the hard knocks that real life has in store?

The answer is a strategy that enlists the Millennials' favorable self-image as a motivator. The new message should be: "Yes, you are special, and we expect special things from you." Moreover: "You'd better do it right, because the whole world is counting on you." This message is successfully employed by community service recruiters, by entry level employers—and by principals of the most dramatically improved K–12 high schools in America. These are schools where every pupil is a "VIP," including early outreach to home and parents, personalized learning plans, individual progress monitoring, and frequent one-on-one meetings with teachers.

Millennials respond well to the message that not only are they special as individuals, but also that they are special as a group. You can appeal to today's youth as a special "generation." A positive collective message about their whole generation will be received much more favorably today than it would have been (by Gen-X youth) in the 1980s or 1990s.

* **Leverage the collective goodwill of the media and public—who are paying close attention to Millennials and their schools.**

In the Millennial youth era, K–12 schools are increasingly becoming a focal point of community activity. Students are spending more time at school after hours and during summers, and voters are spending more time discussing school policies. Parents are also spending more time attending their children's events—and socializing with each other—at school. Since children constitute the strongest tie many of these (Boomer and Gen-X) parents have to the community, schools are increasingly chosen as venues to hold civic meeting and dispense social services to adults. The very archi-

tecture of newly built K–12 schools is changing, away from the age-segregated fortress or industrial look toward an open, friendlier, more casual yet also more adult-like layout that invites people of all ages. According to Patrick Bassett, President of the National Association of Independent Schools, "our schools have become the new town center."

The more intensely the public obsesses over schools, the more important it is for educators to manage that obsession. Bad news can no longer be suppressed or dismissed in today's climate. Almost by definition, anything that goes wrong is a big public story. To whatever extent possible, you can minimize the damage to your school or district by offering full disclosure and offering credible assurances of future improvement. Conversely, good news will spread far and wide and can give schools the opportunity to ask the public for extra support. Excellent state test scores may be the perfect moment to ask for new tax or bond revenue, for special programs donations, or for after-hours volunteering. Good news helps schools overcome a strong current of skepticism about the effectiveness (especially the cost-effectiveness) of public schools.

Schools and districts that have not had much luck reaching out to local civic and business leaders in many years should try again. They may be surprised at the help they now receive, in part because these Boomer and Gen-X leaders are so much more concerned about improving everything that touches the lives of their own children. Most of today's civic leaders agree that the local community revolves around its schools. Most of today's business leaders, who can offer invaluable help to schools (including scholarships, professional expertise, career counseling, job placement, technical training, and "tech prep" programs), likewise see good schools as critical to the future of local economies. A strong alliance with local businesses is especially critical for high school graduates who choose not to undertake or complete a four-year college degree.

6 | Sheltered

"We've become obsessed with safety—bike helmets, car seats, higher drinking ages, graduated driver's licenses. .... Anxiety is the hallmark of modern parenting."

— STEVEN MINTZ, DIRECTOR OF THE AMERICAN CULTURES PROGRAM, UNIVERSITY OF HOUSTON (2005)

Americans have been tightening the security perimeters around Millennials ever since this generation began arriving over twenty years ago. Adults have gradually pulled down per capita rates of divorce, alcohol consumption, drug abuse and other dangers to children. Worried parents have become avid consumers for a booming childproofing industry. According to the 2006 *LifeCourse-Datatel College Parent Survey*, a large majority of parents say they have worked harder to protect their kids from harm than their own parents did for them.

Millennials look up at a castle-like edifice of parental care that keeps getting new bricks added—V-chips and "smart lockers" last month, carding at the

movies this month, graduated licenses and bedroom spy cams next month. Since 9/11, the protective boundaries have drawn even closer, with national TV blaring out "Amber Alert" warnings and "home security" devices that track

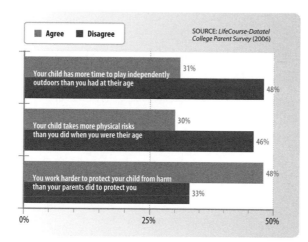

Figure 14 ▶

How Parents
of Millennials
Responded in 2006

teen drivers via GPS. The ever-growing wall of protection is particularly noticeable in schools, from metal detectors to padded playground equipment to post-Columbine SWAT teams. Increasingly, when parents quit jobs, turn down pro-

motions, or opt for flextime to spend more time with their children, their purpose is to keep their children *safe*. Although the demand for private schools is booming, the share of private school parents who choose to board their kids is in steep decline. Nowadays, a private school student is typically a commuting student. These parents either insist on finding a local school or they move the whole family to the neighborhood of their chosen school.

Thus far, Millennials have gone along with little resistance. When sweeping new rules such as student identity cards have been proposed in K–12 schools, the usual experience is initial student resistance, followed by student support once the measures are put in place. By huge majorities, Millennial teens support harsh punishments (including expulsion) for those who misbehave. Extra sheltering would have made Gen Xers suspicious, wondering why adults don't trust them to take care of themselves. But Millennials get the new logic: We are special, therefore we are worth protecting. Suspicion never arises. Gen Xers, who wanted to be seen as tough and self-sufficient, often regarded a visit to a counselor as a form of punishment. Not so Millennials. They welcome the special attention: Sure, I'll see the counselor; the visit will simply make me feel and cope better.

All this sheltering has created a youth generation that is, on the whole, much healthier and less prone to injury and predation than any earlier generation in American history. Federal data show that, between 1988 and 1999, rates of child abduction fell by 23 percent, runaways by 25 percent, substantiated child abuse by 43 percent, and missing children by 51 percent. Name your teen risk: pregnancy, victimization from crime, auto accidents, abuse of serious drugs like alcohol and tobacco, and ingestion of environmental hazards from lead to mercury. All of these risks are dramatically down.

Yet the urge to shelter has also been responsible for some new health problems among Millennials, including the dramatic decline in their physical activity. In 1969, half of all 18-year olds walked or rode a bike to school. Today, kids are six times more likely to play a video game than ride a bike. Meanwhile, physical education classes at schools are being cut back to make room for more academics. Parents don't let their kids outside without supervision for fear of accidents and predators.

Most experts agree that this decline in physical activity has contributed to the tripling in the share

Examples of Child Protection Policies Since 1982

- child restraint & helmet rules
- "child-proof" homes
- blanket Medicaid coverage
- school vaccination checks
- "youth rules" in the workplace
- V-Chips
- social host liability laws
- video game ratings
- Megan's laws
- Amber Alerts
- "graduated" auto licenses
- "cops in shops"
- dragnets for "deadbeat" dads
- urban curfews
- "safe place" havens for kids
- drug-free zones near schools

of children and teens classified as obese, a tripling in the "pre-obesity" rate— and perhaps also to the rising incidence of ADD, ADHD, and asthma. At a time when most youth health indicators are improving, the obesity threat is serious: According to a 2005 article in the *Journal of the American Medical Association*, rising obesity could subtract as many as four to five years from the average life expectancy of today's children. The biggest driver behind this threat is, ironically, the very structured and sheltered style of childrearing favored by today's parents and teachers, which steadily restricts recess, physical education, and unstructured outdoor play.

True to the wishes of adult America, Millennials are protected, feel protected, and expect to be protected—even, some might say, overprotected.

Putting *Sheltered* to Use

✳ **Provide a safe, protected, and "accountable" environment in every school.**

Assure every parent and student that every effort has been made to make their school totally safe. When in doubt, schools are expected to enforce sweeping "zero tolerance" rules to eliminate the very possibility of mischief. The message is as important as the action. Schools not only need to be safe, they must appear safe—with clearly marked perimeters, security personnel with uniforms or visible insignia, and rules prohibiting dress, speech, or behavior that set a dangerous tone.

Surveys show that parental worries about safety have been growing over time, which means that each successive Millennial birth cohort arrives at school facing ever-increasing pressure to avoid danger. Younger (and more market-oriented) Gen-X parents are also demanding "accountability" in a school's safety policies, so that those in charge are held personally responsible if rules are violated and security is breached.

Excessive emphasis on categorical rules can stifle any sense of creative play or risk. Allow school personnel to exercise sensible discretion. Don't forget the importance of teachers setting good examples. And don't get sidetracked into policing every questionable student wordplay or mannerism (which is often mimicked reflexively from the prevailing popular culture). Boys, especially, will respond poorly to draconian rules against any variety of rowdy behavior.

✳ **Define sheltering broadly to include "values" and the seamless delivery of mental health, social, disability, and wellness services.**

The commitment to sheltering must be broad as well as deep. The range of dangers to be guarded against is much more extensive today than when many educators were themselves in school. Now the goal is not just to prevent violence, but also the emotional precursors to violence—such as bullying, physical threats, isolation, malicious gossip, and defamation on

instant messaging or social network websites. Now the goal is not just to deter injury and disease, but to promote wellness—by promoting exercise, sleep, and a better diet, and by providing effective sex education. Protection against harmful "values" is another new frontier, requiring educators to formulate norms on what can be said not only about sex, but about race, ethnicity, religion, and politics.

As many more students with physical and learning disabilities are mainstreamed into today's K–12 classes, and as a growing share of all students are pre-scribed daily medication, every school needs to have disability

The Rise of Small Schools

In *Newsweek's* 1997 list of America's top 100 public high schools (based on college-level test participation) the number of schools with a graduating class of under 100 students was three. By 2007, it had grown to twenty-two. Of the top 5 percent of all public high schools today (roughly 1,300 schools), 20 percent now have graduating classes of under 200.

SOURCE: *Newsweek* (2008)

and healthcare professionals either on staff or on call. Parents and the public at large expect schools to be prepared around the clock.

The dangers posed by the rising rate of obesity among children under eighteen (which has more than tripled over the past thirty years) should be of special concern to schools. As the public begins to mobilize against this emerging new threat, principals and superintendents will be pressed to implement sweeping new policies to change the diet and increase the activity level of their student bodies. The tide is already turning against "pouring rights" for soft drink companies (the extra revenue isn't worth the added calories) and cuts in physical education (the extra academic class time isn't worth the reduction in activity).

✳ **Structure communities that let no one fall through the cracks, with "small classrooms" in primary grades and "small schools" in secondary grades.**

As Millennials have moved through the K–12 school system, educators have started to retool the learning environment to make it smaller, tighter, more structured, more integrated, and more personal. When this generation entered elementary school, small classrooms were the rage. When they moved into middle school, educators introduced learning communities, block scheduling, looped teaching assignments, and team teaching. Many

districts also began to move grades seven and eight back into elementary schools, where the classrooms are smaller and the mood is calmer. When Millennials moved into high school, principals welcomed them with freshmen "houses" and "academies" along with small learning communities (such as career academies) for upperclassmen. Most recently, as Millennials have moved into college, freshmen academies are multiplying there as well—along with "Living Learning Communities" where teams of students actually live with their classmates and with certain faculty.

What do all these innovations have in common? They all provide learning environments in which all students feel they belong and are looked after and in which no student can easily become lost, disoriented, or disengaged. At the extreme, some of the most successful inner-city charter academies constitute a whole new educational approach that David Whitman (in *Sweating the Small Stuff*) calls the "new paternalism"—an approach that allows no activity to be unscripted and no student to be alone or unsupervised. In ways both simple and dramatic, America is creating a carefully protected environment for a carefully sheltered generation.

7 | Confident

"In large part as a result of
their protected, structured,
and positively reinforced
upbringing, the Millennials are
an exceptionally accomplished,
positive, upbeat, and
optimistic generation."

— MORLEY WINOGRAD AND MICHAEL D. HAIS,
IN *MILLENNIAL MAKEOVER* (2007)

"Why are kids so confident?" asked a recent KidsPeace report. "Significantly, the word 'crisis' seems not to appear in the teen lexicon." The Cold War is over. The War on Terror is winnable. And even if the economy flounders, oil prices soar, and the federal budget is deep in the red, at least videogames keep getting cooler, solar cells keep getting cheaper, and grandma and grandpa are well provided for. Millennials are attracted to national leaders who exude a yes-we-can optimism, even if older people sometimes criticize them for what they see as unrealistic "overconfidence."

In 2005, 67 percent of 15- to 22-year olds rated themselves as happy or very happy most of the time. While Boomers, according to the Pew Research Center,

have infused a new pessimism into every phase of life they have entered (most recently, midlife), Millennials are starting out by infusing a new optimism into youth. For over thirty years, until the mid-1990s, the teen suicide rate marched relentlessly upward. Over the last decade, it has declined by 30 percent.

Two years after 9/11, with the economy still struggling to recover, more than half of all teens insisted that "people my age should be optimistic about their chances of having a good job." Today, that bright personal outlook continues. Among youth age ten to seventeen, 95 percent say they "have goals that I want to reach in my life," 92 percent agree that "my success depends on how hard I work," and 88 percent agree that "I'm confident that I'll be able to find a good-paying job when I'm an adult." A rising share of teens (including 95 percent of Latinos and 97 percent of African Americans) believe they will someday be financially more successful than their parents.

The teen view of success has become better rounded and less exclusively focused on one life goal. Over the last decade, surveys show that "marriage/family" and "career success" have each declined in importance as the "one thing" in life. What's become far more important is the concept of balance—between learning and play, and, down the road, between work life and family life. Girls, at the cutting edge of this new generational confidence, are more likely than boys to see how success in school leads directly to success in work and life. Boys, more hesitant and less persuaded by the "powergirl" exemplar, are holding back a bit.

The events of 9/11 and the prospect of related economic shocks have shaken the confidence of many Millennials, but less so than older Americans. More than older generations, these post-Columbine students have grown accustomed to the sight of aggressive security. They are more likely to associate such shows of force with safety (rather than with threats to liberty). In this sense, teenage Millennials appear to be better prepared, functionally and emotionally, for the new mood of post-9/11 America.

Putting *Confident* to Use

✻ Stress positive outcomes for everyone; replace realism with optimism. Have every ninth grader design and follow a "personal progress plan."

do better in college than those who don't take the AP or IB class at all. The bottom line is clear: The old "tracking" walls are crumbling.

* **Address the new challenges with Millennial boys; create contextual, project- and work-based environments for them.**

In the Millennial era, a gap is growing between boys and girls in how well they perform in school and how much they like school. This may be due in part to fewer male teachers (the male share is now at a forty-year low) and the waning of traditionally more boy-oriented activities, such as recess, intra-mural sports, and vocational education classes. More broadly, it is driven by schools' rising emphasis on structure and rules and declining tolerance of risk, both in behavior and in class assignments. Boys continue to do as well as (and often even better than) girls on tests that measure sheer aptitude. But they do worse on any measure of performance that requires engagement and effort—homework, exams, grades, awards, and class participation—and the gap has recently been growing. Boys are also increasingly likely to say they don't like school and don't want to go to college if it is similar to school. This trend may explain why so many boys seem without direction after leaving high school (with or without a degree) and why young men now comprise only three out of every seven college undergraduates.

Educators are responding with a variety of corrective strategies, ranging from single-sex classrooms (offered or required in an estimated 500 public schools, up from fewer than ten a decade ago) to greater sensitivity to the needs of boys in designing behavioral rules and curricula. Above all, they are finding that many Millennial boys respond especially well to project environments such as work-based learning and service- or expeditionary-learning, in which they apply their knowledge to real-world situations and can see how academic skills dovetail with job skills. Career academies are showing differentially greater success (in grades, absenteeism, retention, and college admission) for boys over girls for just this reason.

(Maine) the SAT. The underlying idea is to keep Millennials on track— motivated, energized, and imagining themselves into a successful future.

* Integrate "college-ready" curricula with "school-to-work" applied learning; think win-win.

The new trend in middle and high school reform is to discard the old trade-off between "college prep" curricula and "school-to-work" applied learning. The new attitude is: Let's think win-win. Let's prepare all kids for either option and make every student "college ready," to use the phrase popularized by the Bill and Melinda Gates Foundation.

On the one hand, reformed college prep programs are starting to challenge students to reach beyond academic theories and facts and use their knowledge to solve real-world problems. Project Lead the Way is an innovative example of an engineering and technology curriculum for college-bound students that relies heavily on simulated challenges and design contests. On the other hand, reformed career and technical education programs are starting to introduce academic rigor into their curricula so that what earlier generations knew as "voc ed" curricula now fully prepare students to pursue a two- or four-year college degree. The rapid spread and huge popularity of career academies—small schools for middle and high school students in which the curriculum is structured around career "themes"—proves that mixing relevance and rigor is a winning formula for Millennials and their families.

To determine if a student is ready to take a certain class or perform at a certain level, schools are looking less at the student's aptitude and more at his or her willingness to work hard. The student need not excel in a harder class to benefit from the experience. In fact, research now shows that the difficulty of the courses a student takes in high school (especially math) is highly correlated with the student's later success in college *regardless of how well the student performed in those courses*. A growing number of districts are getting rid of enrollment barriers to their hardest (Advanced Placement or International Baccalaureate) classes. These districts point to data showing that even students who take these AP or IB class and fail the national tests

Confidence in Achieving Career Goals

Asked of high school students:
How confident are you that you will reach your career goals?

Level of Confidence	%
Very confident	62
Fairly confident	31
Just somewhat confident	6
Not that confident	1

SOURCE: *State of Our Nation's Youth*, Horatio Alger Association (2008–09)

With young Gen Xers, schools often tried to describe effective youth programs as "damage control" and counselors often urged students to try second or third career choices in case their first choice was unrealistic. Social marketing to Xers often focused on "scaring kids straight" (in antidrug ads, for example). With Millennials, all this has changed. Today, students insist on following their dream and don't sit still for counselors who won't describe every option as a direct route to a perfect life. Today, the most effective social marketing to youth appeals to positive social norms. Antidrug ads no longer focus on the bad consequences of bad behavior, but rather the good consequences of good behavior, like not letting down your friends or family.

Energize Millennials—and harness this confidence—by having students take concrete actions to plan their future around successful outcomes. Many schools are following the approach originally pioneered by High Schools that Work and now endorsed by the National Association of Secondary School Principals (NASSP), which recommends that every ninth grader be required to draft a six-year career plan (extending two years beyond graduation) and to have that plan regularly approved by counselors and teachers. Some districts now require seniors to fill out college applications. Others encourage seniors to take courses or enroll in local community colleges before graduation. Five states require that all seniors take the ACT and one

8 | Team Oriented

> "They are not individualistic risk-takers like Boomers or cynical and disengaged like Generation Xers. … Millennials are civic minded, trust in leaders, and are team oriented."
>
> — PETER LEYDEN, DIRECTOR OF THE NEW POLITICS INSTITUTE (2007)

From preschool through high school, Millennials have been developing strong team instincts and tight peer bonds. In the Gen-X youth era, educators told students to look after themselves and do everything they could to ensure their own success in life. In the Millennial youth era, educators have been telling students to look after each other and do everything they could to help the community succeed. Through group projects, peer grading, student juries, honor systems, school uniforms, and the like, Boomer educators have encouraged Millennials to acquire the sorts of team habits and civic attitudes that Boomers themselves never really cared for in their own youth.

The new team orientation has broadened Millennials' search for peer friendships, drawing them into circles and cliques. Only three teens in ten report that they usually socialize with only one or two people, while seven in ten do so with larger groups of friends. Kids are transforming information technology itself into a group activity, powering up their IM and email servers as soon as they touch a computer, and making themselves the most 24/7 peer-to-peer "connected" generation in human history. Boomers invented the "personal" computer to get away from the establishment and be creative on their own. Millennials use their PCs to "friend" each other, join groups, and to create large peer communities.

Figure 15 ▶

Share of High School Seniors Who Volunteer: from 1976 to 2007

*1976–2002 for All Seniors, 1985–2007 for Incoming College Freshmen

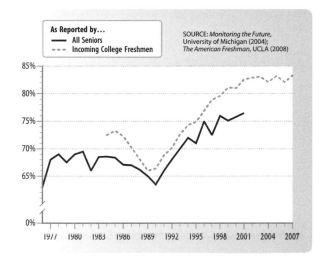

As Reported by...
—— All Seniors
----- Incoming College Freshmen

SOURCE: *Monitoring the Future,* University of Michigan (2004); *The American Freshman,* UCLA (2008)

The increased importance of social groups leads to bigger problems for loners, who may feel comparatively more isolated. A larger share of teens reports being teased about their clothing, and bullying is reported to be a rising problem.

The team ethic is showing up in the new political views of youth. In the 2006 UCLA survey *The American Freshman,* 67 percent of Millennial teens said it is essential or very important to help others who are in difficulty, the highest response in twenty-six years. When teens were asked to identify "the major causes" of America's problems, the number one reason (given by 56 percent of all teens) is "selfishness, people not thinking of the rights of others." Reason number two (given by 52 percent) is "people who don't respect the law and authorities."

Millennials are participating in community service at record rates and are more politically engaged than Gen Xers ever were. Since the Presidential elec-

tion year of 1996, in which only 35 percent of Americans age eighteen to twenty-nine voted, the arrival of Millennials into this age bracket has pushed voter rates steadily higher—to 42 percent in 2000 and to 55 percent in 2004, with even higher percentages expected in 2008.

America's rising income and wealth inequalities are making students increasingly concerned about divisions of money and social class. For some young people, family money is freely available for everything from buying cars to starting careers, but a much larger number do not have these advantages. Given this generation's powerful team instincts, many young people find this issue troubling, and it will likely shape their personal and political agendas.

Putting *Team Oriented* to Use

✳ **Mobilize students in groups; teach team skills; create strong service links to the community. Focus on school "engagement" and "connectedness."**

Back in the Gen-X youth era, many educators disliked peer pressure because they associated the concept with rule-breaking. Today, many are discovering that peer pressure can often be harnessed to enforce rules better. Educators should look for other ways to leverage the Millennial attachment to the group. Because today's students are naturally drawn to communities in which members help each other, make sure that every school-related announcement, symbol, and tradition reinforces this community message. Because they want to participate in some way in their broader regional or national community, establish service programs that let students think of themselves as part of something larger. Because surveys indicate that they believe team skills will be important to their future career success, make sure these skills are explicitly taught.

Educators are paying more attention these days to what Millennial-era reformers call peer "engagement" or "connectedness"—as measured by simple indicators of how well kids get along with each other. Some research indicates that the reason students often learn faster in small-school "house" or "academy" settings has less to do with how well the curriculum is taught than with how well students get along with each other. This research is spurring new attention to engagement among college undergrads and new

interest among college-bound Millennials and their parents in such annual surveys as the *National Survey of Student Engagement.*

Not all educators embrace this growing emphasis on teamwork. Some teachers, Boomers especially, would hesitate to use the extreme peer-pressure tools employed in the most rigorous urban academies, such as the Knowledge Is Power Program (KIPP), Achievement First, and Uncommon Schools—with their uniforms, unison drills, public apologies, and solidarity slogans ("Team Always Beats Individual" is a KIPP favorite). Others regret the phasing out of ability tracking. The mainstreaming of disabled students is still another flashpoint, with many teachers saying that it amounts to "maindumping" by districts that don't want to pay for properly trained specialists. Yet whatever the challenges, nothing is likely to dissuade Millennials from wanting to join inclusive communities. Rather than resist the trend, K–12 schools need to find innovative ways to harness it.

* **Encourage students to lead and organize—and to help other students.**

It's not enough to encourage Millennials to learn and practice team skills. They must also learn and practice leadership skills—which can be surprisingly hard for a generation that has grown up accustomed to following the rules, trusting authority, avoiding social risks, and turning quickly (with the help of texting and IM, if needed) to the group consensus when making choices. Many Millennials hate to seem pushy or self-centered and dislike having to debate each other on sensitive topics—an aversion that often baffles Boomer teachers, who had no such hesitations in their own youth. Yet even a generation that believes in followership—perhaps especially such a generation—needs leadership skills. Schools should teach these skills, and this generation will respond best to learning them in a structured school environment. Millennials need to learn that good leadership is not the same as good followership. It means taking the initiative, thinking creatively about solutions, taking risks when necessary, and not being afraid to speak up.

Service learning provides an excellent opportunity for students to learn teamwork and leadership skills by allowing them to carry out every phase

of a project, from concept and planning to delivery and evaluation. When deciding for themselves which service priorities are highest, Millennial K–12 youth typically choose the needs of other disadvantaged youth, figuring that, since kids are special, helping them must be a good way to serve the community. Youth-helping-youth programs abound. One especially successful program has been Coca-Cola's "Valued Youth Program," which gets at-risk high school students to tutor elementary school students. The positive impact on grades and retention has been dramatic.

* **Turn students into reform allies. Enable them to galvanize support from families, voters, and leaders.**

The early signs suggest that this generation, as it comes of age, will play a much stronger role in mainstream civic activities and electoral politics than their Xer or Boomer parents played at the same age. Millennials are already being encouraged in this direction by their schools and communities, and they may feel further impelled by the relative cynicism and distrust about public institutions they see among Boomers and Gen Xers. Older Americans can already sense this community-strengthening agenda in many of Millennials' early political preferences—to favor consensus-minded leaders, to reject polarizing debate, to stop arguing over racial and ethnic identity, and to start using public policy to rebuild the middle class.

School leaders can leverage the growing civic power and reputation of this generation by showcasing Millennials when it's time to appeal directly to voters and taxpayers for their support. Don't rely so much on older spokespersons. Put the task instead into the hands of a well practiced team of Millennials, who serve as a living embodiment of what our schools do well and of every American's hope for a generation they wish well. Overall adult voting rates rise in districts where Millennials vote on mock ballots in school. Overall family census response rates rise in districts where Millennials fill out mock population forms in school. Americans of all ages are ready to take civic cues from these team-oriented young people when they themselves become the messenger.

9 | Conventional

> "[Surveys] reveal a generation
> brimming with adultlike respect
> for American institutions, family
> values, and work ethics."
>
> — *WASHINGTON TIMES* (2008)

Boomer children felt overdosed on norms and rules, and famously came of age assaulting them. Millennial show signs of trying to reestablish a regime of rules. Their rebellion lies in moving to the ordered center, rather than pushing the anarchic edge.

Why this Millennial move to the center? Having benefitted from a renorming of family life following the turbulent 1960s and 1970s, today's teens no longer feel alienated from the adults who care for them. According to NASSP surveys, eight in ten high school teens now say they have "no problems" with any family member—up from four in ten back in the early 1970s. The share of teens reporting "very different" values from their parents has fallen by roughly

half since the '70s, and the share who say their values are "very or mostly similar" has hit an all-time high of 76 percent.

Behind these trend lies a deeper agreement between students and parents on underlying cultural values—in fact, a virtual closing of the generational culture gap. Millennials trade advice easily with their parents about clothes, entertainment, and careers. They listen to (and perform) their parents' music, share songs with their parents on iPods, and watch remakes of their parents' old movies. Six in ten say it is "easy" to talk to parents about sex, drugs, and alcohol. The special relationship between Millennials and their parents is reflected everywhere in today's culture—even in a popular new line of Hallmark greeting cards that reads, "To my mother, my best friend."

Expert Tools to Help Millennials Plan their Perfect Careers

- Johnson O'Connor Foundation Test (Price: $600)
- Rockport Institute "Path Finder Career Testing Program" (Price: $520)
- Highlands Assessment (administered by local psychologist) (Price: $475)
- The Career Academy, LLC (Price: $295)
- CPP Inc.'s Strong Interest Inventory (Price: $65)

While Millennials are broadly willing to accept their parents' values, they also think they can someday apply these values a whole lot better. They agree by a two-to-one margin that "values and character" will matter more to their own generation as parents. Today's young people are far more trusting of the capacity of large national institutions to do what's right for their generation and for the country. When teens are asked who's going to improve the schools, clean up the environment, and cut the crime rate, they respond—without irony—that it will be teachers, government, and the police. Millennial teens sometimes complain about Boomer parents who get angry about their convictions and paranoid about politics. Most of today's young people gravitate to leaders who seem trusting, consensus-minded, and coolly rational.

As recently remarked by George Gallup, Jr.: "Teens today are decidedly more traditional than their elders were, in both lifestyles and attitudes. *Gallup Youth Survey* data from the past twenty-five years reveal that teens today are far less likely than their parents were to use alcohol, tobacco and marijuana. In addition, they are less likely than their parents even today to approve of sex before marriage and having children out of wedlock." Gallup notes a conventional shift in teen leanings on issues ranging from church-going to abstinence

to divorce. Researchers would not have said anything similar about Boomers forty years ago.

Putting *Conventional* to Use

* **Emphasize a "core" or "essentials learning" curriculum that every student is expected to master, along with core rules that are clear and enforced.**

During the Boomer youth era, schools could energize students by allowing them to break away from the stale "standard" subjects and pursue their own diverse academic interests. Millennials are different: Reacting against the endless splintering of adult opinions and lifestyles, today's students feel empowered by all of the knowledge and skills they share in common. A core curriculum brings students closer together, reinforces a sense of collective mission, minimizes the risk of individual failure, and reassures everybody that they are all progressing and meeting adult approved learning goals.

According to the NASSP, implementing a core or "essential learnings" curriculum can improve a high school by putting the entire student community on a common achievement track. It makes it easier to focus on the critical skills needed in all subjects (like literacy), to introduce innovative teaching methods (like team projects or online aids), and to align the subject matter with the next level of schooling.

Millennials also believe that consistently enforced rules help everyone get more done in school. When asked what are the major problems are in schools today, student regularly put "selfishness" at the top of their list, as well as students (and teachers) who "don't respect" rules and authorities. It's not strict punishment they're after, but simple fairness and an assurance that order is maintained (if necessary, with the removal of the rule-breaker).

* **Make sure that every task is achievable with directed effort; retool learning plans for continuous monitoring, assessment, intervention, and redirection.**

Raised in a structured environment, Millennials require plenty of structure and feedback in their learning. They thrive when they know, day to day, exactly how well they're doing. Some even prefer computerized instruction or computerized essay grading because the computer (unlike the

teacher) automatically senses how well the student "gets" the material and redirects them back to what they don't know. On the other hand, many become demoralized when they embark on big tasks without frequent guideposts. Large open-ended senior term (or "capstone") projects are a growing source of complaints by both students and their parents.

Examine the success story behind any "turn-around" middle school or high school over the last decade and almost surely you will find a new principal who has introduced daily quizzes or weekly progress reports that instantly identify struggling students. Quick corrective action can then be taken, whether a trip to the reading lab, an afterschool session with the teacher, or a conversation with parents. With the help of course management systems like Edline and Blackboard, the scheduling of special appointments is automatic and all interested parties (including parents) are notified daily. With the help of electronic clickers, teachers in some schools can now get classroom feedback from students in real time—while each class is still in progress.

During the Boomer youth era, teachers typically gave exams simply to evaluate students at the end of coursework—and Boomers often thrived in unstructured classes where exams were regarded as an afterthought. In the Millennial youth era, step-by-step monitoring has become more important. Indeed, evaluation has become an integral part of the teaching process itself.

✻ **Implement reforms that involve parents, community, and friends, and allow "regular kids" to celebrate their progress.**

Enable Millennials to see school as part of a balanced life that includes close connections to their friends, family, and community. Don't be deterred by Boomers and Gen Xers who roll their eyes at rah-rah school spirit. Millennials enjoy "stepping up" ceremonies at which they can formally celebrate their progress in the presence of their peers. They are pleased to keep mom and dad updated on their activities. And they are inspired by traditions and stories that connect their school with the past and future.

A growing number of schools are rediscovering the efficacy of what educator and author Terrence Deal calls the "values, loyalties, rituals, and stories" that motivate today's students to see their efforts as part of something

larger than themselves. Even older Americans accept that businesses may need to issue "mission statements" or brighten their "workplace culture." Why not schools as well?

As the profitability of awards companies like Jostens attests, Millennial ceremonies typically involve a multitude of trophies, ribbons, stars, plaques, and buttons—a glittering waterfall of adulation that some adults worry gives rise to unrealistic expectations. These worries are misplaced. Millennials understand that most prizes reward participation more than excellence and are intended to bolster group morale more than single out individuals. Indeed, one strong trend in the Millennial youth era is to replace awards that used to go to one individual (one valedictorian, one homecoming queen, one science fair winner, and so on) with awards that go instead to groups.

10 | Pressured

"When I graduated from high school in 1994, we could take classes for enjoyment and not worry about how it would look on a transcript. Today, many kids can't take classes like music, photography, journalism, or yearbook because they fear they will fall behind in class rank."

— ALEXANDRA ROBBINS, IN *THE OVERACHIEVERS* (2006)

Stress has become the daily reality of Millennials' lives. Their new digital technologies place more demands on them. Their schools place more demands on them. Most importantly, their own ambitions (and their parents' ambitions for them) place more demands on them.

The new youth assumption that long-term success demands near-term organization and achievement sometimes overwhelms Millennials. What a high school junior does this week determines where she'll be five and ten years from now. That, at least, is the new teen perception—and it's a reversal of a forty-year trend. Most Millennials watch classic Gen-X films like *Ferris Bueller's Day Off,*

Fast Times at Ridgemont High, and *Wayne's World* with amusement, to be sure, but with little or no self identification.

Rather than breed a sense of entitlement, the rising public demand for higher achievement standards has placed Millennial students into a pressure cooker. The growing flood of well credentialed high school seniors increases competition for the best college slots. Technology, with its incessant stream of emails, instant messages, and text messages, puts still more burdens on kids' time. To help themselves cope, students are multitasking like never before. An MTV survey of how much time teenagers spend on various activities added up to twenty-six hours each day—not including sleep. Since the mid-1980s, "unstructured activity" has been the most rapidly declining use of time (as measured by daily time diaries) among primary school kids.

Figure 16 ▶

Homework Time
as Reported by
10th-Graders:
Hours per Week,
in 1980 and 2002

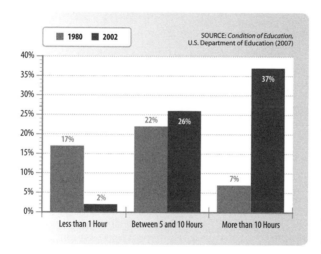

From the earliest grades forward, constant pressure keeps many Millennials moving, busy, and purposeful. Kids as young as six are now extensively drilled, tested, and evaluated. Middle school students receive formal instruction in time management, buttressed by such best sellers as Sean Covey's *The 7 Habits of Highly Effective Teens*. The number of state reading and math tests has more than doubled from 253 in 1996 to 600 in 2006. Three-fourths of public schools now begin before September first. A growing share of students are assigned summer assignments and reading lists or enroll in summer school to keep up with (or get ahead of) peers, rather than to remediate. To be sure, many K–12 students remain stuck in poor schools that fail to supervise, interest, or challenge them. But a rising share of these disadvantaged Millennials tell pollsters that they *do* care about

Stressed Out Students

In 2008, 45 percent of U.S. high school students agree that the pressure to get good grades "is a major problem for me"—up from 26 percent in 2001. Four-fifths say they plan to enter college immediately after high school, and over a third say they have started or will start to search for colleges by their sophomore year. Fifty-nine percent complain that they do not get enough sleep. Nearly 30 percent say they fall asleep at least once a week doing homework, and about the same share say they are too tired to do any type of physical exercise. According to one regional survey of high school students in the San Francisco Bay Area, nearly two-thirds feel "often" or "always" stressed by school work. Twenty-five percent use stimulants like Red Bull or NoDoz; 9 percent use prescription drugs like Adderall.

SOURCE: *State of Our Nation's Youth,* Horatio Alger Association (2008–09); *2006 Sleep in America Poll,* National Sleep Foundation (2006); Stanford Bay Area Teen Survey, as cited in *Wall Street Journal* (May 24, 2008)

their future and that they wish they *were* challenged—if only someone would take charge.

Millennials do well under pressure—but pressure (like sheltering) can sometimes be excessive, with negative health consequences. Time pressure prevents most Millennials from getting enough exercise, while some are pressured to overspecialize in a single sport, leading to the rise of repetitive stress injuries. Emotional distress that leads to life-threatening behaviors (suicide, violent crime, heavy substance abuse) is declining. But the frequency of eating disorders, sleep deprivation, "smart drug" use, and cutting is rising—as a rising share of youth try to cope with stress through obsessive rituals of self control.

To many Millennials, it's as though a giant generational train is leaving the station. Either they're on the platform, on time and with their ticket punched, or they'll miss the train and never be able to catch up.

Putting *Pressured* to Use

✻ **Stress long-term life planning and guarantees over short-term opportunities and risks.**

Millennials are used to pressure and don't mind the heat so long as they are assured that all the careful energy they invest will someday be rewarded. Educators should stress long-term rewards over short-term payoffs.

Many Boomer and Gen-X counselors do not understand this shift. Boomers, in their youth, heard G.I. counselors tell them they should build their careers carefully and prudently, step by step—advice that many

Boomers promptly rejected in their efforts to defy the "system" and find themselves. Gen-X youth took this impulse one step further and crafted a whole free-agent ethic that focused exclusively on taking risks and cashing in on momentary marketplace opportunities. Millennials are moving in a different direction, in part because they have witnessed the later-in-life downside of their parents' choices (such as no job security, no health benefits, and no pension).

Today, Millennials are disconcerted to hear so many Boomers and Gen-Xers tell them not to worry, to take risks, and to expect to make many mistakes before they know what they want in life. Millennials don't want to take risks. They want to plan perfect careers from the very beginning. Upon graduation, more and more of them aim to pursue degrees, credentials, and internships that will plug them into quality employers who will guarantee them a future—even if it means living for the time being with mom and dad. The situational "McJob" ethic of the Gen Xer finds few Millennial followers—which explains why part-time employment is now in steep decline among teens and why temp work is in steep decline among adults in their early 20s.

✳ **Structure all learning (and grading) around mastery of goals. Backward design the curriculum accordingly.**

To fire the imagination of Millennials, don't describe education as a process in which subjects are merely "covered." Instead, promise a journey whose end stage is the mastery of every skill they need to succeed at the next level. Then follow up on this promise by restructuring the curriculum to throw out everything that doesn't help students get to this destination and to strengthen everything that does. The National Association of Secondary School Principals refers to this as "backward designing" the curriculum: Start with a vision of the kind of student you want upon graduation and then reshape the coursework step by step to get everyone there. Most schools that rigorously implement this approach discover that much classroom time had been wasted and that many hours per week could be allocated to more useful tasks.

Most Millennials are energized by the idea that school is all about moving them toward known and measurable goals. Yes, they still feel pressure, but now they know what they need to do to be successful—and so do the teachers and staff who now share with students a common sense of urgency. After finding out that nine in ten middle school kids want to go to college but only three in ten know what courses are required by colleges, the Lumina Foundation funded a "pathways to college" campaign and a "KnowHow2Go" website that shows teens which steps they need to take and in what order. Older generations are sometimes uncomfortable with so much emphasis on measurable goals, which seems to translate into mere test prepping. But as former Colorado Governor and Los Angeles School Superintendent Roy Romer famously pointed out, "there is nothing wrong with teaching to the test" if the test is good enough "to define where you want to go."

✳ **Emphasize alignment everywhere—for schools, coursework, and teachers—and closely articulate secondary with postsecondary education.**

Pay careful attention to alignment between levels. With the overwhelming majority of teens saying that they fully expect to get some sort of postsecondary degree, Millennials do not lack aspirations. What they often do lack, tragically, are schools that can satisfy those aspirations. A great many school districts have never taken a hard and objective look at whether students exiting one level of schooling are prepared for the next. A recent national ACT survey, for example, shows that on average three-quarters of high school educators believe they are preparing students "very well" for college-level work—but only *one-third* of college educators agree. In certain states and regions, the gap is surely much wider.

Quite simply, many schools are satisfied with an off-ramp that comes nowhere near the next on-ramp, and these are precisely the gaps where Millennials are most likely to stumble, get overlooked, and fall out of the system. Ninth grade is when most students drop out of high school, and freshman year is when most undergrads, swamped in remedial ed, drop out of college. This misalignment was less of a problem for self-reliant Gen-X youth, who probably didn't put a lot of trust in the school system to begin

with and sooner or later found their own way. It is a much bigger problem for Millennials, who do trust the system and expect proper signage on their road to the future.

To realign the curriculum, most states have now initiated P-16 councils. School systems should reach out and welcome these efforts—especially offers from state and community colleges to meet with high school administrators and provide orientation and alignment training to high school teachers. High schools should look carefully at their freshman year and make certain (perhaps in a small school "academy" setting) that freshmen are receiving sufficient orientation and their fair share of quality teachers. The transition to college can be improved by expanding "accelerated learning options" (like tech prep, early college, and dual enrollment) that give juniors and seniors plenty of contact with college-level work.

11 | Achieving

"These kids have ambition and
aspiration coming out of their
ears. They want to be leaders
when they grow up. They
want to change the world."

— *NEW YORK TIMES* (2007)

Every year, the highest-achieving Millennials astound older Americans by showing off their academic prowess. In the twentieth century, the National Spelling Bee could be won with words like *knack* (1932), *therapy* (1940), *vouchsafe* (1973), or *lyceum* (1992). In the new millennium, the winning words include tongue twisters like *succedaneum*, *prospicience*, *pococurante*, *autochthonous*, *appoggiatura*, *ursprache*, and (the 2007 winner) *guerdon*.

With higher school standards rising to the top of America's political agenda, Millennials are taking academic achievement seriously. Most high school students today support standardized testing and higher standards, and believe that the best cure for rampant classroom boredom is a tougher curriculum. By vast majorities, they agree that "being smart is cool."

Algebra is now taught in many elementary schools, and trigonometry in many middle schools. While No Child Left Behind does not require states to adopt a national achievement standard, many states are opting to do so on their own. Thirty-two states have signed on to Achieve Inc.'s American Diploma Project, committing themselves to raising the bar to a common standard, and nine states are using a common exam for Algebra II. A growing number of states require students to pass specific course exams in order to graduate. A rising share of high school students are taking college prep courses (from physics to calculus). Students and parents alike now fret over proliferating lists of the "best schools," charter options, and expensive tutoring services. Over 400,000 public high school students now take courses for college credit, and over the last decade the annual number of AP exams with a score of three or better has doubled for white students and tripled for minorities.

A much higher share of Millennial teens of both sexes say they aspire to postsecondary education than the teens of any prior generation. Over seven in ten of today's high school students say they are aiming for a four-year college degree, and solid majorities of all races and ethnicities agree that a college degree confers "respect." According to the 2006 *LifeCourse-Chartwells College Student Survey*, Millennial teens agree by a ten to one margin that having a college degree is "more important" for them than it was for their parents. Many teens who today want degrees may in time discover they lack the motivation, education, or money necessary to get them. Even so, this generation as a whole will be more inclined to let their best and brightest set the cultural tone than Boomers or Gen Xers were in their own coming-of-age years.

Showing a left-brained tilt, Millennials demonstrate more interest and improvement in math and science than in the arts or social sciences. They report that math and science are their "hardest" subjects yet also, tellingly, the subjects they "enjoy the most." Meanwhile, girls are taking a clear lead in academic achievement over boys, who (say teachers) may have the smarts but are less likely to do the work or make the effort. In today's more achievement-oriented climate, work and effort are what count—which helps explain the growing female advantage in college admissions.

Academics are hardly the whole picture. When you add their harder-to-measure but equally important accomplishments outside of the classroom, the Millennial bottom line is very impressive. Student publications, government, sports, music, theater, clubs, and community service are getting better every year.

Today's young people know this. They have a high regard for their own generation, which they see has a powerhouse full of high achievers, no matter what some politicians or op-ed writers might say about them. Day to day, this is less a matter of glowing pride than a constant source of personal pressure for kids to not fall behind all of their achievement-minded peers.

Putting *Achieving* to Use

∗ **Keep standards and expectations high. Keep every student challenged, directed, and empowered—not just in academics but also in extracurriculars.**

Remarkably, a more challenging curriculum actually improves Millennial retention and graduation rates. According to Public Agenda, four out of five high school students agree that summer school should be mandatory for students who cannot meet higher academic standards. A full 50 percent of black students (and 30 percent of whites) agree that "academic standards are too low, and kids are not expected to learn enough." Surveys of recent high school dropouts indicate that two-thirds would have worked harder "if more had been demanded of me."

The old wisdom: Dumb down the curriculum to make it easier for more students, especially the disadvantaged, to move along and graduate. For Millennials, the new wisdom is: Charge up the curriculum and turn a vicious cycle of boredom and disengagement into a virtuous cycle of accomplishment and focus. Early and middle college programs, which enroll at-risk students (mostly boys) in college-level courses, have been successful precisely for this reason.

This rising emphasis on achievement is also changing the rules of the game for the most talented college-bound youth. Ten or twenty years ago, applicants applying to a good college could appeal to many criteria: effort, aptitude, alumni status, and racial preference, just to name a few. While still important,

all of these are now under attack. They are losing ground to national benchmarked exams that focus exclusively on academic achievement—such as APs, the IB, and SAT IIs—or on life stories or extracurriculars that demonstrate personal achievement. Even the SAT I has been recently retooled to emphasize subject mastery over raw "ability." Certifiable achievement, something everyone can work and plan for, is rapidly becoming the universal standard for college admission—and for accolades from other Millennials.

* **Integrate cutting-edge networked information and communication technologies (ICT skills) into the curriculum whenever possible.**

Surveys confirm that Millennials are well aware that information and communications technology (ICT) breakthroughs will transform society and the economy during their lifetime—and that, as a generation, they are likely to play a key role in steering this transformation. As the most 24/7 peer-to-peer connected generation in world history, Millennials also sense that they can use ICT to reinforce their powerful sense of teamwork. Today, Millennials are building virtual social communities with mobile phones, texting, IM, Twitter, MySpace, and Facebook. Twenty years from now, they may be building virtual political institutions with software that hasn't yet been invented. To invite students to use ICT in their academic lives (they are already using it in their personal lives) is therefore to give them a headstart in what they perceive as a critical life mission.

Don't just invite Millennials to use ICT. Invite them to innovate and improve it, perhaps by allowing classes to invent their own teaching games or animations to help master a difficult subject. Most ICT innovation is nontheoretical and project based. This makes it an excellent way for schools to make their (disproportionately male) noncollege youth feel they can keep up with their (disproportionately female) collegiate peers.

* **Focus on objective achievement goals and get everyone—teachers, students, families, and communities—involved in meeting them.**

"It's the journey, not the destination." So goes a favorite saying among Boomers who, when young, shunned establishment goalposts and wanted

to follow their own compass. A new generation is now rising and the tables are now turned. Boomers and Gen Xers need to understand that for Millennials, it's *not* about the journey and it *is* about the destination—and that what Millennials want most from older people is real assistance getting them there. Schools can help get parents involved by informing them very clearly about what their children need to do in order to succeed and by keeping them current with their children's performance. They can help get communities involved by informing them very clearly about how student success will impact the economic and social future of the region.

Schools can also help get teachers more involved—by impressing on teachers (along with all other school personnel) the importance of setting a personal example of the achievement ethic they are urging upon their students. To this end, schools should initiate and foster active communities of practice that allow teachers to discuss methods, curriculum, and students with each other, sit in on each other's classes, and keep up with statewide and nationwide innovations in their specialty subjects. Teachers routinely tell students that, in today's flat-world global economy, they must be "life-long learners." For the message to stick, teachers themselves must embody this ideal. It is not enough simply to be a good teacher. Truly good teachers are those who try each day, like their students, to become better.

PART THREE

Other Generations in K-12 Schools

"The adults who staff our schools—teachers, principals, guidance counselors, librarians, custodians—come from four distinct generations. ...The characteristics and idiosyncrasies that members of each of these generations bring into the schoolhouse have an extraordinary influence on the day-to-day life of the school and on its culture."

— ROLAND BARTH, IN FOREWORD TO *GENERATIONS AT SCHOOL* BY SUZETTE LOVELY AND AUSTIN G. BUFFUM (2007)

As Millennials age through childhood and graduate from high school, older generations are maturing as well, in ways that are also having a major impact on K–12 schools.

We look first at the recent shift in the dominant generation of parents—from Boomers, who came of age in the 1960s or 1970s and raised most of the early-wave Millennials, to Gen Xers, who came of age in the 1980s or 1990s and are raising most of the late-wave Millennials. Gen-X parents are different from Boomer parents. They are obtrusively protective of their kids. They distrust all big institutions, including schools. They bring with them a new focus on accountability, transparency, and choice.

We turn next to the generational turnover happening within K–12 schools. Boomers are ascending to senior positions as board members, superintendants, and nonprofit executives. Compared to Silent administrators, they are focused less on process and consensus, and tend to focus on values and ideas, and are often considered workaholics. As Gen Xers replace Boomers as the dominant generation of teachers, they take flexibility for granted and focus on the bottom line. Compared to Boomer teachers, they are less about depth, professionalism, and the work ethic—and more about breadth, innovation, and the market ethic. Meanwhile, a new generation of Millennial teachers is just now coming

on board. To retain the best Millennial teachers, K–12 schools need to employ many of the same strategies they use to motivate the best Millennial students.

Finally, we look ahead to a new, post-Millennial generation of children—we call them the Homeland Generation—who will shortly be entering kindergarten and first grade. Time marches on. A few years from now, elementary schools will be puzzling over a new batch of kids who are as different from Millennials as Millennials are from Generation X.

12 | The Generational Lineup

"You belong to it too. You came along at the same time. You can't get away from it. You're part of it whether you want to be or not."

— THOMAS WOLFE, ON HIS OWN "GENERATION," IN *YOU CAN'T GO HOME AGAIN* (1940)

A social generation is often defined as a group that consists of everyone born over the span of a single phase of life (roughly twenty years) and that shares a collective peer personality. A peer personality is forged by many forces—most importantly, by a common age location in history, by common attitudes and behavior traits, and by a common collective identity that gives rise to generational names like "Boomers" or "Generation X." By this definition, Millennials clearly comprise a generation. And so do earlier-born Americans, who all belong to generations of their own, each with boundaries that are just as firmly marked by when they came along, by who they are, and by how they see themselves.

What does it means to belong to a generation? It does not mean that we necessarily identify with or even like our own peer group. But it does mean

that our bedrock beliefs, our assumptions about life, our daily habits, and our collective sense of self are strongly shaped by our formative years, and thus by our generational membership.

Like any social category that helps define who we are (race, class, or nationality), a generation can allow plenty of individual exceptions and be fuzzy at the edges. Yet unlike most other categories, it possesses its own biography. You can tell a lifelong story about the shared experiences of the Silent Generation in ways you never could for all women, all Hispanics, or all Californians. The reason, wrote Ortega y Gasset, is that a generation is "a species of biological missile hurled into space at a given instant, with a certain velocity and direction," which gives it a "preestablished vital trajectory." A generation can feel nostalgia for a unique past, express urgency about a future of limited duration, and comprehend its own mortality. As Martin Heidegger once observed, "the fateful act of living in and with one's generation completes the drama of human existence."

Let's now turn from Millennials to America's older living generations, each having its own "vital trajectory." As the first half of the Millennial Generation moves out of classrooms and the second half moves in, the aging of older generations will trigger several other decisive transitions. These will involve parents, voters, teachers, and school executives and have a seismic impact on K–12 schools.

G.I. Generation

Our country's oldest living generation is the G.I. Generation (born 1901–24). The G.I.s were raised as kids during the Progressive Era and the Roaring Twenties and came of age during the Great Depression and World War II. In midlife, they built suburbs, invented vaccines, laid out interstates, and launched moon rockets. Civic-minded and politically powerful all their lives (even deep in old age—think of the AARP), G.I.s built many of the bedrock postwar social and economic institutions that younger people take for granted. That includes the standardized K–12 school system and "comprehensive high school." The G.I.s themselves were a generation of extraordinary educational achievement (see box on "Grading Older Generations"), and they hoped to institutionalize that success in a system that would guarantee steady educational progress for

their own children and grandchildren. Those hopes ran aground, for better or for worse, when Boomer and Gen-X students passed through that system in the 1960s, 1970s, and 1980s.

Today's elder generation of "senior citizens," G.I.s remind younger educators that once upon a time most people trusted schools, respected teachers, and believed that national progress depended upon a well-run "school system." Perhaps that time will come again. But because G.I.s today no longer have any important influence on K–12 schools, their aging and departure will not figure in our projections.

Famous G.I.s

Walt Disney, Judy Garland, Charles Lindbergh, Sidney Poitier, John F. Kennedy, Richard Nixon, Ronald Reagan, Jimmy Stewart, Ann Landers, Henry Kissinger

Silent Generation

Coming along after the G.I.s is the Silent Generation (born 1925–42). The Silent grew up as the seen-but-not-heard children of global war and economic depression. Their first wave came of age just too late to be World War II heroes and their last wave just too early to be youthful free spirits. Instead, this early marrying "lonely crowd" became the risk-averse technicians and professionals as well as the sensitive rock 'n' rollers and civil rights advocates of a post-Crisis era—an era in which conformity seemed to be a sure ticket to success.

Midlife was an anxious passage for a generation torn between stolid elders and passionate juniors. Their assumption of national leadership, in the 1970s, coincided with fragmenting families, cultural diversity, institutional complexity, and too much litigation. Many of them, believing that their own (depression- and war-era) childhood had been too strict and sheltered, chose much greater freedom for their own late-wave Boomer and early-wave Gen Xer kids. The Silent are now entering elderhood with unprecedented affluence, a hip style, and a reputation for indecision.

The Silent passed through elementary and secondary schools during the 1930s and '40s, when teachers took for granted that children would behave well, work hard, and follow the straight and narrow path to success. As educa-

tors, they set the tone for the nation's schools during the late 1960s through 1980s. Often allying with like-aged culture heroes (including Bob Dylan, Ken Kesey, Richard Prior, Joan Baez, and Jerry Rubin), Silent educators took the lead in dismantling G.I. rules, diversifying requirements, and experimenting with "open classrooms," independent learning, and unstructured curricula.

As K–12 parents, they were generally hands-off, content to sit back and let the school system do its work. Skillful with discussion and "process," many Silent educators continue to preside over school bureaucracies while mediating among their younger colleagues. But most are now retiring from their positions as school officials, board members, and superintendents.

Famous Silent

John McCain, Joe Biden, Martin Luther King, Jr., Nancy Pelosi, Richard Cheney, Sandra Day O'Connor, Colin Powell, Dan Rather, Shirley Temple, Elvis Presley, Bill Cosby, Paul Simon

Boom Generation

Everyone has heard about the Boom Generation (born 1943–60). Boomers grew up as indulged youth during an era of community-spirited progress. As kids, they were the proud creation of postwar optimism, Dr. Spock rationalism, and *Father Knows Best* family order. Coming of age, however, Boomers loudly proclaimed their antipathy to the secular blueprints of their parents; they demanded inner visions over outer, self-perfection over thing-making or team-playing.

The Boom "Awakening" climaxed with Vietnam War protests, the 1967 "summer of love," inner-city riots, the first Earth Day, and Kent State. At roughly the same time, SAT scores commenced their seventeen-year fall, reflecting a steady decline in measured educational achievement at all grade levels along with a steady rise in rates of antisocial behavior (from drug abuse and teen pregnancy to suicide and violent crime). By the early 1980s, Boomer "yuppies," many of them now into cocooning and "family values," appointed themselves arbiters of the nation's values. They crowded into such "culture careers" as teaching, religion, journalism, marketing, and the arts. During the '90s, they trumpeted values, touted a "politics of meaning" and waged scorched-earth culture wars.

First-wave Boomers passed through schools during a time of strong community and civic confidence, when the teaching profession—dominated by well-educated, glass-ceilinged G.I. women—was at a height of public prestige. By the time the last wave arrived, schools were immersed in a raging controversy over social turmoil, youth anger, and worsening outcomes. Boomers flooded into teaching careers in the 1980s and '90s, bringing an intensive work ethic and an ideological bent. As parents, they have been an active, supportive, and hovering group, viewing public schools as institutions of mission and meaning and colleges as essential destinations for their own children. They now comprise the vast majority of superintendents and are at their peak of influence in universities and in political leadership.

What are they doing with this authority? The same generation that once demanded "unconditional amnesty," pass-fail courses, and a "don't fold, spindle, or mutilate" anti-computer ethos is now imposing zero tolerance, more homework, and a wide array of tests on their own children.

Famous Boomers

Bill and Hillary Clinton, George W. and Laura Bush, Oprah Winfrey, Bill Gates, Condoleezza Rice, Tom Hanks, Meryl Streep, Rush Limbaugh, Katie Couric, Steven Spielberg.

Generation X

Generation X (born 1961–81) survived a hurried childhood of divorce, latchkeys, open classrooms, and devil-child movies. They learned young that they were largely on their own—and could not count on any institution, including schools, to watch out for their best interests. As young adults navigating a sexual battlescape of AIDS and blighted courtship rituals, they dated and married cautiously. In jobs, they have embraced free-agent risk and trust the marketplace over institutional intermediaries.

From grunge to hip hop, their culture has revealed a hardened edge. Politically, they have leaned toward pragmatism and nonaffiliation, and many would rather volunteer than vote. Widely criticized as "slackers," and facing a *Reality Bites* economy of declining young adult living standards, they have

embodied the resilience of post-9/11 America and have matured into one of the most dynamic generations of entrepreneurs in U.S. history.

Gen Xers passed through grade school while the Consciousness Revolution was in full boil. Even as their school achievement leveled out, *The Nation at Risk* report accused them of being "a rising tide of mediocrity." Teachers' pay declined dramatically, in-school supervision was curtailed, and the teaching of "the basics" was deemphasized.

As today's dominant teacher corps and rising generation of political leaders, this market-oriented, "just do it" generation is moving away from ideology and bringing a new focus on productivity and measurable standards. Gen-X graduates of Teach for America include most of today's hardest-edged K–12 reformers—including Washington, DC, public school chancellor Michelle Rhee and KIPP founders Dave Levin and Mike Feinberg. As parents, Gen Xers are determined not to let their children experience the same problems they recall from their own childhood years. They have provided the most vocal constituency for school reforms that set standards, require transparency, impose accountability, and enable all forms of parental choice, from home schooling to vouchers to charter schools.

Famous Gen Xers

Barack Obama, Sarah Palin, Michael Jordan, Tom Cruise, Michael Dell, Jon Stewart, Jodie Foster, Kurt Cobain, Julia Roberts, Johnny Depp, Quentin Tarantino, Jay-Z, Jeff Bezos

13 | The New Gen-X Parent

> "City by city, homegrown 'parents for public schools'-style websites are springing up daily, little rebel force fires on the horizon. …What my Gen X sisters and I have inherited from the Boomers is not a better world, but a blasted public education and community landscape. …Picture us hurtling about not in creamy Volvos but in Mad Max/Road Warrior trash cars. Ours are the kids who will only play soccer if we personally hand-stitch the soccer ball, nail up the goalposts and put shovel to field."
>
> — SANDRA TSING LOH, AUTHOR OF *MOTHER ON FIRE: A TRUE MOTHERF%#$@ STORY ABOUT PARENTING*, IN *THE WASHINGTON POST* (2008)

Over the past decade, Gen Xers have been taking over from Boomers as the majority of K–12 parents. In the early 1990s, a growing share of Gen Xers began filling Parent Teacher Associations (PTAs) in the nation's elementary schools. Around 2005, they became the majority of middle school parents. In the fall of 2008, they are finally taking over as the dominant parents of high school seniors.

Gen-X Parents: How They Are Different

Gen-X parents and Boomer parents belong to two neighboring generations, each possessing its own location in history and its own peer personality. They are similar in some respects, but clearly different in others.

Like Boomer parents, who have passionately supported stricter protection and higher academic standards in schools over the past quarter century, Gen-X parents are also strongly committed to sheltering their kids and to improving the curriculum. But their motives and priorities are not the same. Gen Xers are much less likely to trust schools in their day-to-day operation than Boomers. Also, Gen-X parents are much more likely than Boomers to say they are protecting their own kids and pushing them to succeed more than their own parents protected or pushed them. This means that Gen-X parents tend to be more deliberate, intrusive, hands on, and even rude about how they pursue their kids' perceived interests. Gen Xers, unlike Boomers, often seem to expect failure from schools—and feel energized by making sure what once happened to them won't happen to their own children. As the *Washington Post* recently quipped, "Parental involvement in our schools has become an extreme sport."

While many Boomers say that their Millennial children *complete* their sense of life mission, more Gen Xers say that their Millennial children *are* their life mission. A rising share of parents with school-age children are planning their whole lives around these children—for example, moving to costly neighborhoods only for the sake of the schools. Married Gen-X women are now leaving the workforce to be with their kids. Married Gen-X dads are spending a rising share of their week with them. The social status of the "stay-at-home" parent, in gradual decline since the 1970s, is once again on the rise. Gen-X parents who work full time are demanding more flexible hours, in part to spend more time with their children.

Parents Who Move to Get Better Schools

In 2003, the parents of 24 percent of K–12 students reported that they moved to their neighborhood primarily to have their child attend better schools or a specific school. For parents of public schools only, the share was 28 percent, with a still higher share for parents of urban public schools. Otherwise, the number varies little by race, ethnicity, income, or educational level of parent.

SOURCE: *Condition of Education,*
U.S. Department of Education (2007)

The Boomer-Xer
Parental Difference

Parents' Generation	Agree (%)	Disagree (%)
You spend more time with your child than your parents spent with you.		
Boomer	51	31
Xer	57	21
You work harder to protect your child from harm than your parents did for you.		
Boomer	43	37
Xer	52	28
You push your child harder to do well in school than your parents pushed you.		
Boomer	43	36
Xer	53	24

SOURCE: *LifeCourse-Datatel College Parent Survey* (2006)

At the same time, Gen Xers are less focused than Boomers on demanding abstract perfection, for schools as institutions, for themselves as parents, or for their own kids as students. Gen Xers don't care as much if the school is safe for everyone, so long as it is safe for their own child. Meeting lofty academic standards are less essential, so long as their own child has a direct and tangible path to his or her own secure career. With their instinct for low-sweat pragmatism, the Gen-X parent avoids spending time and money on missions that have no personal payoff (and may be unachievable, anyway). What they prefer is the easiest and most direct path to success, especially a path that gives both the parent and the child extra time to just goof off and have fun.

The whole image of the workaholic supermom (or "soccer mom") created by Boomers in the 1990s—the sort of mom who demands the best of everything—is in disrepute among Gen Xers. According to the Boston marketing firm Reach Advisors, in a report entitled *Generation X Parents: From Grunge to Grown Up*, today's younger moms want to focus more on what their kids absolutely need and less on everything else. The most popular recent childcare guides put more emphasis on correcting behavior and avoiding harmful mistakes, and less on correcting emotions and instilling high aspirations. Gen

Xers believe that good parents who succeed in making the right basic choices (about safety, neighborhood, school, influencers, and so on) can otherwise be casual "buddies" with their kids. They sometimes talk about "protection from pressure." They are less likely than Boomers to believe that good parenting requires extraordinary credentials (notice the rising popularity of "Parenting for Dummies" book titles) or that a good parent must always be worrying and in charge.

Now let's be more specific. Compared to Boomers, Gen-X parents are:

* More personally attached, protective, and directive of their children.

Throughout the 1990s, educators grew accustomed to "helicopter parents," Boomer parents of Millennials who are sometimes helpful, sometimes annoying, yet always hovering and making noise. Today, behold the era of the Gen-X "stealth-fighter parent." Stealth-fighter parents do not hover; they choose when and where they will attack. If the issue seems below their threshold of importance, they save their energy and let it go entirely. But if it crosses their threshold and shows up on their radar, they will strike— rapidly, in force, and often with no warning.

When these Gen-X "security moms" and "committed dads" are fully roused, they can be even more protective and interventionist than Boomers ever were. Web junkies, they will monitor Edline and Blackboard sites nightly, email board members, trade advice on blogs, and look up teacher credentials. Flex workers, they will juggle schedules to monitor their kids' activities in person. Speedy multitaskers, they will quickly switch their kids into—or take them out of—any situation according to their assessment of their kids' interests.

* More oriented toward their own kids when voting and volunteering.

Boomers have always cared deeply about the higher moral and civic goals of education, for the ultimate purpose (recall the sixties!) of creating a more ethical and socially conscious community. By contrast, Gen-X moms and dads tend to be more interested in the private purposes of education, in how the right school will create concrete opportunities for their own chil-

dren. Many Gen Xers believe they live in an individualistic world in which there is no common interest and people do best by looking out for their own interests. As voters, they are less sympathetic than Boomers to cross subsidies and state equalization formulas and more intent on preserving local funds for local purposes. As parents, they will be better informed about their own child's achievement and less informed about how other children are doing. Where Boomers, for example, might be perfectly happy in volunteering for a district-wide curriculum committee, Gen-X parents will be more enthusiastic about helping out in ways that directly benefit their child's own class or allow them to personally monitor their own child's activities, as a class trip chaperone, for example.

✱ **Less trusting of educators and less idealistic about education.**

Whereas Boomer helicopter parents generally assume that the rewards of school and college are vast but impossible to measure, stealth-fighter parents are more likely to assume that anything immeasurable is untrustworthy—and maybe just a feel-good con job. Back when Xers were graduating from K–12, one blue ribbon commission after another told them that their schools had failed and that the passionate hopes of '60s reformers had miscarried. Now they want proof that their children won't have the same problem, and the proof they demand has to be something better than good intentions—empirical evidence, for example. Many Gen-X parents acquire a surprising degree of (self-taught) expertise about teaching methods and will bring stacks of Web printouts into meetings with teachers. A quip often used by Education Secretary Margaret Spellings (herself a very late-wave Boomer, born in 1957) speaks to many Gen-X parents: "In God we trust. All others bring data."

The local, pragmatic, bottom-line perspective of Gen Xers certainly contrasts with the more global, idealistic, and aspirational perspective of Boomers. It has driven the rapid growth of parent-teacher organizations (PTOs) that opt out of any affiliation to the National Parent Teacher Association (PTA). According to many younger parents, the PTA is simply too large, too inflexible, too politically correct, and too deferential to the

educational establishment. Many older k–12 teachers and administrators describe Gen-X parents as more "conservative." In certain respects, the term obviously doesn't fit: Gen Xers talk a lot more about what they want to change about schools than what they want to "conserve." Yet in other respects, it does reflect the shifting political orientation of a generation shaped more by the Reagan 1980s than by the Movement 1960s.

✳ More sensitive to price and more insistent on "choice."

Skeptical of grandiose claims and worried (sometimes even desperate) about making ends meet economically, most Gen Xers are acutely sensitive to the prices they pay and the value they receive in return. As voters, they can be easily persuaded to doubt that a routine tax or fee is really worth whatever schools are buying with it. As parents, they comparison shop to make sure that a school's reputation or brand is really worth all the life costs they must incur (including mortgage payments and property taxes) for their children to go there. They are always looking for a discount or shortcut. While Boomers may brag about how much they paid for a BMW, Gen Xers are more likely to brag about how *little* they paid.

As a whole, Gen Xers feel comfortable with market outcomes. Compared to other adult generations, they are underrepresented in the public sector and large corporate workforce (where market forces are weak) and over-represented in the small business and entrepreneurial workforce (where market forces are strong). Most Gen-X parents, accordingly, expect schools to be run like customer-oriented businesses. As with other purchases and investments, Gen Xers believe their children's education should be a fair and open transaction with complete and accurate information and uncon-strained consumer choice. They will evaluate the transaction on the basis of the value it appears to offer. If it doesn't offer the right value, they will take their business elsewhere—whether another school district, a charter school, a private school, or home schooling. It is practically impossible to persuade most Gen-X parents that they should relinquish their choice for the sake of some great public good.

✳ **Less patient and respectful as problem solvers.**

Administrators have long complained about Boomer helicopter parents who argue endlessly with teachers and administrators whenever their child encounters a problem. Gen-X stealth-fighter parents are less likely to argue at great length and more likely to find a loophole, buck rank, or go quickly to a confrontational posture, which may include ultimatums or even unfriendly words or gestures. Some Xers may even skip the discussion stage entirely and move immediately to a decisive action—suddenly filing a lawsuit, for example, or withdrawing their child from a school with no warning. Less inclined than Boomers to think that persuasion will work, they will often inform a school after their decision is already made. Employers have already noticed this difference with Gen Xers as employees. When they don't like their boss, they don't talk, they walk. As K–12 parents, they will walk with their child.

Gen-X Parents: How Schools Can Respond

So how should schools adjust to this broad shift in generational attitudes and priorities? Educators can implement the following strategies to handle Gen-X parents:

✳ **Assume no trust, market to them, spell out rules, and
start relationships early.**

To win over Gen Xer consumers, almost every industry—from cars to health plans to financial and legal services—is trying to build trust by assuming no brand loyalty, by rejustifying product value from the ground up, and by educating buyers about what they must do and must not do in order for the product to work as expected. K–12 schools will get along better with Gen-X if they take a similar approach.

First, assume no trust. Given their generally positive or at least empowering experience with educational institutions, Boomers have generally trusted the school bureaucracy to do right by their children. Not today's younger parents. Schools must gird themselves for Gen Xers who feel they have no reason to trust the schools' competence—and schools must take

steps (in print, on websites, and in parent briefings) to justify their performance in every area, from physical safety to academic achievement.

Second, market to them. More business oriented than Boomers, Gen Xers are impressed by marketing skills that enable an institution to make its best case quickly and easily to busy consumers. Incredibly, public school districts routinely bury favorable findings about their performance in unreadable memos, while allowing the media to shape negative findings without rebuttal. Most districts would benefit by hiring at least a marketing consultant. To Gen Xers—who disproportionately fill the ranks of America's sales and marketing workforce—the inability to shape and project a clear message is itself a symptom of incompetence.

Third, spell out the rules. Gen Xers, accustomed to thriving in a high-option, freewheeling marketplace, tend to believe that they have a right to anything not explicitly denied them in the contract. When introducing themselves to parents, K–12 districts should explicitly spell out the reciprocal obligations of parents and schools—and enumerate concretely where the school will take the lead (and parents should not interfere) and where parents must pitch in to ensure student success. Like many colleges, schools can frame this agreement as a "contract" or "covenant." While not legally binding, this document will arrest the attention of Gen-X parents who always want to know the rules of the game.

Finally, schools should make every effort to start their relationship with parents early and on their own terms before there is a problem. For parents who may be distrustful to begin with, an initial meeting at which all the parents' concerns are aired will make a big difference if their child ends up failing an exam or being suspended for misbehavior. The teacher or councilor could be an ally in whom the parent confides—or an enemy whom the parent fights tooth and nail. The first meeting often makes all the difference.

✳ **Stress personal accountability and personal contribution.**

Compared to Boomers, Gen Xers are less likely to trust good intentions or a well-designed institutional process and more likely to trust bottom-line incentives and personal accountability. Gen-X parents don't want to see

guidelines and flowcharts outlining a school's emergency response plan or curriculum acceleration plan. What they want to see is a real person who is concretely accountable for the outcome—someone who has skin in the game, so to speak. School leaders should stress a chain of personal accountability for anything that goes wrong, particularly in "zero-tolerance" areas like school safety. Designate a go-to person for everything from fire drills to hall-monitoring to student counseling and mental health.

Showcasing accountability will help win over Gen Xers, who in their own market-oriented lives are accustomed to bottom-line incentives (win this contract and get a bonus, lose it and you're fired), and are often suspicious of institutions where individual accountability never seems to enter the picture. A similar approach will help draw Gen-X parents into volunteering for tasks that don't involve their own children. Give them "ownership" of the project. Make sure they understand that they are helping real people, not just "the system." And find creative ways to reward them if it goes well, as many of these parents are entrepreneurial.

✱ **Offer data, standards, transparency, and return on investment (ROI).**

Gen-X parents want measurable standards for schools, teachers, and students. They want to know how those standards are linked to career and life success. They want to see data measuring the achievement of those standards. And they expect transparency in all important deliberations about strategy. Xer constituents will call on school boards to show in detail that they are getting a return on their investment—that each tax dollar serves a concrete purpose for their children's education. They are less likely than Boomers to accept credentials (of schools, administrators, and teachers) at face value, and will want access to data on everything from hiring practices to teacher evaluations.

Gen-X parents will be especially prone to swivel their stealth-fighter targeting devices toward issues that affect student success. Schools will face rising pressure to offer accurate and comprehensible information on all their evaluation systems—from consistency in grade point averages and Advanced Placement (AP) scores across schools and courses to procedures for assigning

class levels and evaluating disabilities. Above all, educators should collect data on what happens to students after they leave their halls. Gen-X parents are often astonished to find out how little schools know about student outcomes after graduation. They are familiar with the marketplace, in which companies are judged—continuously and without mercy—according to how well their products measure up. Gen-X parents will demand more than graduation and college enrollment rates. They will want to know the documented career outcomes and earnings capabilities of graduates five and ten years down the road. They may also want to see data comparing long-term outcomes among a diversity of choices—such as "stopping out" of school for a year, home schooling, entering a career academy, loading up on AP courses, using community college as a stepping stone for a four-year degree, and so on. Gen Xers want to advise their child in the same way they manage their finances: hands on, eyes open, all options on the table.

✳ Offer real-time service (the "FedEx" test).

Gen-X parents will apply the "FedEx" test to their children's schools, expecting the service to be cheerful, fast, and efficient, with information and options in real time, online, 24/7. As educators are already beginning to note, once-per-semester parent teacher nights, snail-mail notifications, and rotary phone messages will no longer cut it. If Gen-X parents can get instant, real-time information on something as trivial as a package, why should they stay in the dark about their child's academic performance? School leaders should use digital technology to offer parents continuous access and include them in a tight cycle of intervention and redirection whenever their children hit an educational snag. Course management systems like Edline, which allow teachers to record and track each student's performance every day, can also be used to share performance data instantly with parents. Some years down the road, when fewer Boomers are left to object, schools may even install real-time video monitoring systems that let parents tune in to whatever is happening in their child's classroom.

* **Enable parent choice; present your school as the best option in a competitive market.**

Ever since their children first began to enter elementary school, Gen Xers have been the most vocal constituency for educational policies that empower parent choice, including vouchers, magnet schools, and home schooling. Even within the public school system, the share of parents who say they "choose" (rather than being "assigned to") their public school has grown steadily—from 11 percent in 1993 to 15 percent in 2003 and 18 percent in 2007. If anything, the trend is accelerating.

Public school leaders who have grown accustomed to their role as default educators will no longer enjoy this luxury. Both public and private school leaders need to market their schools as a top-notch option in a competitive education market and be able to persuade parents that they do indeed deliver the goods. Gen Xers like being informed and energetic consumers. When Gen-X parents perceive that they are really choosing a school, their enthusiam and goodwill can be beneficial. When they perceive they don't have any real choice, on the other hand, educators should prepare for a strong backlash over any policy event (such as a decision to close down or combine schools or to redraw district lines) that reinforces their sense of being "trapped." Boomers, while often complaining, usually end up accommodating themselves to whatever the system dishes out. Gen Xers are more likely to fight tooth and nail and even "game the system" in order to send their child to the school that they decide is best.

* **Prepare for the modular "opt-out" consumer and the innovative high-tech competitor.**

Gen Xers like to compartmentalize, viewing every transaction as a menu-driven series of discrete and modular choices. Across America, Gen-X consumers are dealing out the middleman, avoiding product "packages," and demanding that every item be customized to their tastes. Why buy a whole CD when you can purchase just the one song you like on iTunes? Similarly, when making educational choices for their children, they are likely to won-

der why they should sign on for the whole K–12 package when some parts of it may not be a perfect fit for their special child.

Many will want to split the K–12 experience into its components and pick and choose exactly what they want for their children. If a high school student wants to take a course that is not offered, can he take it online or at a community college, for credit? If a middle schooler is passionate about fencing, can she opt out of physical education to take lessons? If she wants to study marine biology, can she attend the career academy across town in the afternoons? If a student drops out, is there a customized, high-tech substitute to get that high school degree credential? If a certain school fails to facilitate this level of customization, Gen-X parents will take their business and their children elsewhere.

As Gen-X parents generate a rising demand for a wide spectrum of educational choices and credential substitutes over the next couple of decades, other Gen Xers entering midlife are likely to rise up to meet this demand. Gen-X entrepreneurs will find ways to provide new options outside the traditional school setting—for example, through auxiliary programs, online courses, career modules, and homeschooling aids. Gen-X infotech designers will steadily improve the efficacy, flexibility, interactivity, and entertainment value of teaching tools. Meanwhile, as Gen-X voters, executives, and elected officials replace Boomers in top leadership roles, they may agree to relax the credentials and help legitimize these end runs around the system. K–12 schools can deal with these new options by working with them, adopting them, or outcompeting them. They cannot simply ignore them.

In the coming era of accountability, K–12 leaders need to face up to the rising tide of Gen-X parents. Schools that figure it out, collect the right data, and market themselves intelligently to this new generation of parents will be able to rebrand themselves for success in the decades ahead.

14 | Changing Generations of Teachers and Leaders

"Generation Xers bring a fresh approach to the teaching profession and are not inhibited by existing rules and regulations. Xers are not afraid to leave an organization if they are unhappy. … They possess strong individualism and are not afraid to go it alone. … Xer teacher leaders also will move their schools into complete dependence upon technology."

— HOWARD C. CARLSON, IN "CHANGING OF THE GUARD," *SCHOOL ADMINISTRATOR* (2004)

At any time, people across a wide range of ages have key roles in K–12 education—from 5-year old preschoolers on up. Teachers tend to range in age from their twenties through their fifties. Administrators tend to be a little older, school boards and trustees older still.

Today, Millennials constitute the entire K–12 and traditional college-age population, and have recently begun to join the ranks of brand new teachers. Gen Xers account for more than half of K–12 teachers and are a small but growing share of school administrators. Boomers are the older K–12 teachers

(including those on the brink of retirement) and most of the administrators. Their influence on K–12 education is at its peak and will soon start to wane.

What does this generational lineup mean for schools? As younger generations replace older ones in each role, the overall mood and direction of K–12 schools will shift dramatically, and in predictable ways. This will create a number of key issues for educators to address.

Top Leadership: Boomers Replacing Silent

The Silent Generation set the tone in K–12 schools from the mid-1960s through the mid-1980s, shepherding hardscrabble Gen-X children through an era of consciousness revolution upheaval. They are now retiring from their reigning positions as board members, superintendents, and active leaders of civic organizations. This generation of educators has had a penchant for process and retains a deep trust in committees, supervisory boards, and other bureaucratic tools. They are less likely than Boomers to take strong ideological stances and more likely to listen to and mediate the passions and conflicts of their younger colleagues.

As Boomers take over K–12 leadership and Silent influence wanes, schools will feel the full impact of aggressive Boomer agendas in curriculum and values, unsoftened by Silent moderation and compromise. Boomer leaders may intensify the culture wars over everything from curriculum and discipline to school choice and budget priorities. Gen-X teachers will appreciate the greater passion that Boomers bring to their leadership role and will join with Boomers in their quest to reform the bureaucracy and throw out any mindless old-school rules. But they will not appreciate the way Boomers, in their visionary quest to reshape society and instill deeper values, often pay insufficient attention to defining success, measuring outcomes, pursuing efficacy, improving productivity, and restraining cost. To many Gen Xers, high ideals is a Boomer strength, but common sense is a Boomer weakness.

Teachers: Gen Xers Replacing Boomers

Given their very different peer personalities, it is no surprise that Boomers and Gen-X teachers tend to have broadly different styles and priorities. As Xers

take over from Boomers as the dominant generation of teachers, schools will see these differences emerge in full force.

Compared to Boomers, Gen-X teachers:

* **Have a weaker work ethic, but a stronger market ethic (principles vs. productivity).**

Famous for their passionate pursuit of "callings," Boomers in general— and Boomer teachers in particular— are more likely than professionals in other generations to describe themselves as "workaholic." They are often willing to put in extra hours for special projects, whether paid or not, as a reflection of their personal dedication and principles. Gen-X teachers

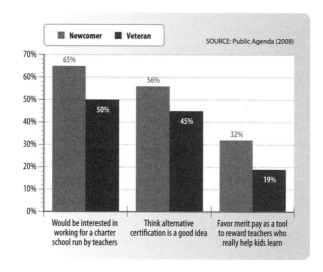

■ Newcomer ■ Veteran

SOURCE: Public Agenda (2008)

- 65% / 50% — Would be interested in working for a charter school run by teachers
- 56% / 45% — Think alternative certification is a good idea
- 32% / 19% — Favor merit pay as a tool to reward teachers who really help kids learn

◀ **Figure 17**

Attitudes of Older vs. Younger Teachers, in 2008

bring a more bottom-line outlook to the workplace: Get the maximum productivity out of your job with the minimum toll on your personal life. While Boomers take pride in their work ethic, Gen Xers are more likely to subscribe to a market ethic. While Boomers use words like "career" and "vocation" to suggest that their work *is* their life, Gen Xers are more likely to use words like "job" or "assignment" to suggest that work is simply how they *get* a life. Younger teachers chafe when asked to put in extra hours "on principle," often a source of conflict between them and Boomer bosses.

Contrary to what Boomers may think, Gen-X teachers are not lazy or "slackers"—they simply value accountability and execution over process and principles. Most of them want to know that any extra work really generates concrete results for the ultimate consumer, the students and their

families, and they are comfortable with direct incentives that push teachers toward that end. Gen-X teachers are therefore more likely than Boomers to embrace market-oriented reforms, such as voucher options for parents, incentive pay for schools and teachers and flexible scheduling, alternative credentialing, and unconventional job switching for all K–12 personnel. They are more comfortable with rapid job turnover. They are less committed to teachers unions and less tolerant of differences in pay and prestige that seem unrelated to measurable on-the-job performance.

✳ **Have less depth, more breadth.**

Boomers have a penchant for delving deeply into one subject area and single-mindedly pursuing whatever issues spark their passion. They tend to develop a deep, substantive understanding of the subjects they teach, and many have spent years developing a well of knowledge that goes far beyond the textbooks. Gen Xers more often prefer breadth rather than depth, browsing online at Wikipedia or through "Idiot's Guide" books on random subjects rather than relying only on peer-reviewed journals or formal coursework. The generation that invented the question "will it be on the exam?" is skeptical that great depth will really be all that helpful. Xers figure that that breadth will prepare them for a greater variety of situations. While not matching the Boomers' deep knowledge, they are more willing to take on new subjects, to welcome high-tech teaching tools, and to bring a multidisciplinary perspective to their teaching. Shared innovative video resources like *teachertube.com* and *schooltube.com* are almost entirely Xer-produced and Xer-consumed. Boomers are apt to feel that, because these tools are free and fun and unregulated, there must be something wrong with them.

✳ **Have less professionalism, more flexibility.**

Many Boomer teachers are personally committed to education as an idealistic calling, or at least consider themselves strongly attached to a serious profession with its own history, theory, scholarship, and time-tested methodology. This passion and dedication means that many Boomers can be brilliantly effective teachers, but it also means that others find it difficult

to accept feedback or to reassess their performance when their methods don't work. Gen-X teachers, whose "just in time" attitude often triggers Boomer criticism, aren't as serious about their profession per se. They are more likely to have entered teaching through alternative credentials, to move to another district or specialty in search of a better teaching opportunity, and to consider future jobs outside of teaching altogether. For these very reasons, Gen Xers are more likely to accept criticism and to embrace change. They find it easier to step outside themselves, look at their performance objectively, and take corrective action.

When radical teaching reforms are under consideration, Gen Xers are usually more open to arguments and data indicating the superiority of a

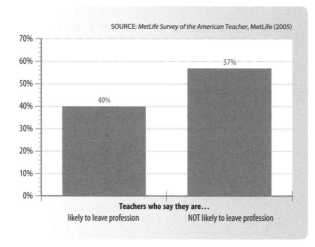

SOURCE: *MetLife Survey of the American Teacher*, MetLife (2005)

Teachers who say they are...
likely to leave profession — 40%
NOT likely to leave profession — 57%

◀ **Figure 18**

Percent of K–12 teachers who agree: "At my school, there is cooperation among more experienced teachers and new teachers."

new method. When these reforms are put to a teacher vote (as they often are), Gen Xers are usually more supportive than Boomers—particularly when they involve heavily programmed, "direct instruction" routines. Boomers take offense at any effort to curtail their creative and professional autonomy. Xers are more likely to say: If it works, let's try it. Having no affinity for many of the grand progressive causes that once kindled the idealism of Boomers, Gen-X teachers see nothing wrong with pragmatism.

✳ Are less independent, more collaborative.

Gen-X teachers are not exactly team players by nature. But because they aren't as zealously protective of their professional privilege and creative independence as Boomers, they are more open to collaborative teaching styles. Gen-X teachers are disproportionately drawn to small learning community

environments that feature team teaching, looping, block scheduling, and common planning time. They tend to be less bothered by letting other teachers or parents sit in on a class. Always eager to broaden their skill set, they tend to be more enthusiastic about joining communities of practice to share information and advice. At some schools, the divide between group teachers and solo teachers is essentially a generational gap between Xers and Boomers. Once it appears, this gap can be destructive. Schools in which younger teachers feel they have little support or communication with older teachers experience higher rates of turnover. When both generations work closely together, though, everyone gains. Gen Xers learn from Boomers (about mastering the curriculum, for example), and Boomers learn from Gen Xers (about technology, for example, or about how to handle Gen-X parents).

Now Arriving: The New Millennial Teachers

Over the last few years, the first cohorts of Millennials have been coming back to school—this time as the newest crop of entry level teachers. This post-X rising generation will change the teacher corps in many of the same ways that they have changed student bodies. Indeed, workplaces across every sector of the economy have been noticing a Millennial shift in the attitudes and behaviors of young employees.

As the next generation of teachers, Millennials will:

✳ Expect to be treated as VIPs.

Just as Millennial students expected to be treated as special, so do Millennial job seekers. Yet the slow pace and impersonal feel of the public school hiring process sends exactly the opposite message. Schools should contact young recruits personally, match them with veteran teachers to answer their questions, and expedite the application process. Offer special orientations and ongoing mentoring to new hires. Comarket job opportunities to Millennials' parents, who remain highly involved—from updating a parents' portion of your website to giving parents details of a job offer.

* Assume they are protected.

The era of the *in loco parentis* employer has arrived. Much as they have done for Millennial students, schools will be expected to take institutional responsibility for protecting young teachers across all aspects of their lives. Keep transparent data on employee risks and do everything possible to minimize them. Provide a comprehensive envelope of support and guidance on life basics, from emotional counseling to relocation assistance to navigating healthcare.

* Have long-term goals.

Millennial students often have five- and ten-year plans—and, as young workers, they continue to take a long-term perspective on their lives and careers. Schools should position themselves as durable partners in achieving young teachers' career aspirations. Offer extensive in-house training and skill development and showcase a variety of paths for improvement or advancement. Woo first-wave Millennial recruits (and their worried Boomer parents) with newly important long-term benefits like retirement plans and life insurance.

* Thrive with structure and feedback.

Millennial teachers prefer a structured work culture with clear expectations and tight cycles of feedback, mirroring the rule-bound world they have lived in from kindergarten on up. Schools should provide detailed schedules, job descriptions, and instructions for following the curriculum. Offer detailed performance reviews and frequent (even weekly) "check-ins" so young teachers know they are on the right track. Provide abundant structure, support, and mentoring for the new teacher's initial classroom experience. Millennials will not respond well to the sink-or-swim classroom rite of passage experienced by so many young Boomer and Gen-X teachers.

* Work best in teams and want to help their community.

As Millennials enter the workplace, they are bringing their collaborative style with them. Leverage young teachers' strengths by offering bonding

retreats, group skills development, and peer mentoring. Strengthen lines of communication between teachers and administrators. Give them social networking tech tools, including laptops with IM and Twitter software. Appeal to recruits' new sense of civic engagement by emphasizing teachers' positive impact on the community.

15 | Next Up: A "Homeland" Generation of Students

"Parenthood, market researchers say, is turning the 'Whatever' generation into hyper-vigilant homebodies."

— *THE WASHINGTON POST* (2008)

The Homeland Generation (Born 200?, age ?) is probably arriving now in America's nurseries. Though is still too early to set their first birthyear (this will be clear in time), we do know that they will comprise nearly all of the babies born between now and the mid-2020s. Their always-on-guard nurturing style will be substantially set by Gen-X parents, legislators, and media producers. Already gaining a reputation for extreme sheltering, Xer stay-at-home dads and "security moms" will not want to see their own children relive the *Dazed and Confused* childhood they recall from the 1960s and '70s. The protective rules initiated for the Millennials will become customary, no longer controversial. Homelanders will receive "total situation" childcare, surveilled

by digital-mobile technology, emotionally screened by psychological software, and guarded from inappropriate media through entertainment controls. At the same time, public attention to and celebration of children, now at its peak, will begin to drop. The adult world will turn its attention to larger public problems as structured methods and institutions point out the "easy way" to raise kids and keep them safe.

From first cohort to last, increasing parental protection has been a strong trend for Millennials. Now that last-wave Millennials are passing the generational baton to first-wave Homeland toddlers, the hypersheltering of kids is now fully in place. Insisting that no unknown substance touch their babies' skin, Gen-X parents are generating a multimillion dollar market for baby gear that is free of chemicals like phthalates and bisphenol A. They shop for BPA-free baby bottles and stainless steel "safe sippies." They are fueling the fast-growing demand for organic baby food, buy low-VOC paints for their babies' rooms, and opt for chemical-free mattresses. Expectant moms go on extreme "whole baby" diets before "scheduling delivery" at just the perfect (and most convenient) time.

At-home Xer moms and dads are starting blogs where parents trade secrets about how to sew GPS chips into their child's clothing or where to buy the best long-sleeved U/V protective swimsuits. At-work Xer moms and dads are demanding credentialed childcare of ever-increasing quality. All Xer parents are reading childcare guides that have become brutally prescriptive, with short lists of do's and long lists of absolute don'ts. They pass these lists on to Silent and Boomer grandparents who, when caring for these small children, tremble lest they make a mistake. The friendly, reassuring tone of Dr. Spock's guide is ancient history. High-income parents celebrate their precious children, in Xer-like fashion, with pregnancy spas, and brand name baby carriages and toys—a trend that has been called "blinging up baby." Low-income parents place new emphasis on constant parental contact, even if it means having the baby near while they work. If *quality* time was the Boomer mantra for Millennials, *quantity* time is the Xer mantra for Homelanders.

The objects of all this protection will grow up well behaved, diligent, and imaginative—but also somewhat passive, naïve, and emotionally fragile. They

will come of age eager to please adults, avoiding the unorthodox, keeping their heads down, and safeguarding their "permanent records." Those marked as "problem children" will not, like their Gen-X parents at that age, be kids who commit crimes or act wild so much as kids who do nothing—who refuse to take advantage of all the opportunities offered by their protective elders.

As Homelanders pass through schools, education will become increasingly programmed, rule bound, and results oriented. A preview of what's to come can be seen in today's young late-wave Millennial children, who are already more heavily drilled, tested, and evaluated than ever before. Sales of learning software and "Leapfrog" educational toys are soaring as parents race to start their children ever earlier on the straight and narrow path to success. Highly-scheduled children are turning to "Time Trackers" to remind them to do their next task. Many educators now favor behavioral regimens that teach small kids "self-regulation" skills (these include "releasing," "focusing," and "dial-setting") as an antidote for ADD and overall rowdiness.

Reformers today tout "universal prekindergarten," and some states are already making public preschools available to all parents. Kindergarten, once play based, has become the new first grade, while first grade has become a literacy boot camp that can even include mandatory summer school. Junior Kumon, a nationwide tutoring program created for children as young as two years old, covers math and reading. No-nonsense obedience is on the rise as preschools eliminate naptime and expel children for bad behavior. By the time Homelanders enter schools over the next few years, they will encounter a secure, rule-bound, and some might say smothering world.

Graduation and Beyond

"As is the generation of leaves, so too of men:
At one time the wind shakes the leaves to the
ground but then the flourishing woods
Gives birth, and the season of spring
comes into existence
So it is with the generations of men,
Which alternately come forth and pass away."

— HOMER, IN *ILIAD, BOOK VI*

When educators contemplate today's rising generation of Millennials, they are aware that much of what Boomer and Gen-X teachers impart to them is an investment that will bear fruit only after the teachers themselves have passed away. And this points to a question: Should it matter to us what generations do after we're gone?

Yes, it should—considering how far our lives extend backward and forward through time.

Let's assume that you're a Boomer teacher, born in the early 1950s. Consider, for a moment, the oldest person who influenced you as a child—and then the youngest child you are likely to influence when you are old. Add these lifetimes together and you get something we call your family memory span.

How long is this span? Well, odds are that you had a grandmother or grandfather who was born in the 1880s and that you hope to have and know a grandchild who will live well into the 2100s. That's over 220 years. That's the long time: 220 years is nearly as long as the United States has been a nation.

Millennials are only the fourteenth generation of U.S. citizens since the first U.S. generation of Ben Franklin and Sam Adams. Their collective lifespan may dominate the twenty-first century as much as the World-War-winning G.I. Generation dominated the 20th. So as we look at this new generation, let's look not just at who they are, but at what they will become. And let us not be surprised if what they become changes history.

16 | The Next Great Generation

> "This is a new generation that sees itself at the forefront of a great movement, just like the greatest movements of the past."
>
> — MILLENNIAL ACTIVIST JESSY TOLKAN, *TIME MAGAZINE* (2007)

Every generation has its own strengths and weaknesses, its own potential for triumph and tragedy. The course of human history affords to each generation an opportunity to apply its unique gifts for the benefit of others. Some generations steer society toward outer-world rationality, others toward inner-world passion. Some focus on graceful refinement, others on the hardscrabble bottom line. The German historian Leopold von Ranke, who weighed many Old World generations on the scales of history, observed that "before God all the generations of humanity appear equally justified." In "any generation," he concluded, "real moral greatness is the same as in any other..."

What will Millennials provide for those who come after? It is this future contribution, not what they have done in youth, which will be their test of greatness.

The collective Millennial lifespan, and its influence on history, will stretch far into the twenty-first century. In 2000, the first cohorts graduated from high school. In 2002, they began graduating from college with associate and professional degrees. In 2004, they began graduating with Bachelor degrees. In 2006, they began graduating from business and professional schools, in 2007 from law schools, and in 2009 they will begin graduating from medical schools and Ph.D. programs. Over the next two decades, this generation will continue to fill the ranks of young adult celebrities in the Olympics, pro sports, and entertainment—and the ranks of the military in any wars the nation may wage. In 2007, the first Millennial women reached the median age of first marriage and of giving birth to a first child. The first Millennial men will reach that age in 2009. From now through 2020, Millennials will make a major mark on the youth pop culture. A new youth activism has already begun to have a real impact on national politics in the 2008 presidential election, and this impact will grow even stronger in the 2012 election.

Through the 2010s, Millennials will be giving birth in large numbers, returning to high school for their tenth-year reunions, and swarming into business and the professions, no longer as apprentices. Some will enter state houses and the U.S. Congress. Around 2020, they will elect their first U.S. Senator; around 2030, their first U.S. President. In the 2010s, their children will begin filling K–12 schools. They will occupy the White House into the 2050s, during which period they will also provide majorities in the Congress and Senate, win Nobel prizes, and rule corporate board rooms. Thereafter, into the 2070s, they will occupy the Supreme Court and be America's new elders. Along the way, they will make lasting contributions to literature, science, technology, and many other fields. Their children will dominate American life in the latter half of the twenty-first century—and their grandchildren will lead us into the twenty-second. Their influence on the American story, and the memory of their deeds and collective persona, will reach far beyond the year 2100.

As is true for any generation, history will intrude on the Millennials' collective life story, posing distinct challenges and opportunities. How they respond will alter the way others see them and the way they see themselves. What would one have said about the future of the G.I. Generation of youth back in 1928, before World War II and the New Deal redefined who they were and how they lived their lives? What would one have said about the future of young Boomers back in 1962, before the Consciousness Revolution? And what of Generation X in 1980, before deregulation and the digital age?

Toward the close of his renomination address in 1936, President Roosevelt said:

There is a mysterious cycle in human events.
To some generations much is given.
Of other generations much is expected.
This generation of Americans has a rendezvous with destiny.

When summoning "this generation" to a "rendezvous with destiny," Roosevelt may have been referring specifically to the G.I. Generation—those young men and women who had overwhelmingly voted him into office and who, within a few years, would rally behind his elder leadership with dedication, energy, courage, and intelligence. Together, all of America's adult generations—leaders, generals, and soldiers—fought and won a war civilization could not afford to lose, achieving a triumph we today honor with monuments and memorials.

Perhaps because we know them better than the two other World War II-era generations, we especially revere today's very old G.I. war veterans and their widows. As young people, the G.I.s understood how much older generations had given them. They wanted to give back and they did, by fighting courageously in World War II, and also by nurturing a new postwar generation of idealistic Boomers. Those Boomers have given birth to the first Millennials, and the story continues.

The Millennials' greatness as a generation has yet to reveal itself. When the strengths of this generation do appear, it is unlikely they will resemble those

of their Boomer parents. Instead, their virtues are more likely to call to mind the confidence, optimism, and civic spirit of the high-achieving G.I.s.

What will happen over the course of Millennials' lives is, of course, unknowable. If they face their own "rendezvous with destiny" as they come of age, much will be expected of them by older generations. Will future writers have reason to call them, on their record of achievement, another "great generation"? Time will tell.

As was true in Roosevelt's time, educators will play an important role in preparing young people for whatever they may encounter. Beyond catering to Millennials' personal needs—in academics, in the workplace, in the culture, in families—educators can keep in mind what is likely to be required of them by history. Beyond considering students' own aspirations, consider what will be expected of this rising generation by society, the nation, and the world—and what their own "rendezvous with destiny" might in fact be.

Millennials are rising. And, with them, so may the service to history of today's educators.

About the Authors

For twenty years, Neil Howe and William Strauss have been best-selling authors, national speakers, and renowned authorities on generations in America. They have together written six books, all widely used by businesses, colleges, government agencies, and political leaders of both parties. *Millennials and K–12 Schools* is based on earlier articles that the authors have co-written about generations and education. William Strauss passed away in December of 2007, before this book was published.

Howe and Strauss's blend of social science and history and their in-depth analysis of American generations lend order, meaning, and even a measure of predictability to social change. Their theories and predictions are based on their profiles of generations—each reflecting distinct values formed during the eras in which its members grew up and came of age. The authors have observed that similar generational profiles recur in cycles driven by a rhythmic pattern of non-linear shifts, or "turnings," in America's social mood. This cyclical pattern has been present for centuries, and not just in America. History shapes generations, and then generations shape history.

Howe and Strauss's first book, *Generations* (Morrow, 1991), is a history of America told as a sequence of generational biographies. *Generations* has been photographed on Bill Clinton's White House desk, quoted approvingly by Rush Limbaugh and Newt Gingrich, used by Tony Robbins, and cited by economic forecasters from Harry Dent to David Hale. Then-Vice President Al Gore sent a copy to every Member of Congress, calling it, "the most stimulating book on American history I have ever read."

Their second book, *13th-Gen* (Vintage, 1993), remains the top-selling non-fiction book on Generation X. *The Fourth Turning* (Broadway, 1997) forecast

a major mood change in America shortly after the new millennium—a change much like what actually happened after September 11, 2001. *The Fourth Turning* reached number ten on the *amazon.com* list four years after its release, and its web site (*fourthturning.com*) hosts the internet's longest-running discussion forum for any nonfiction book. "We will never be able to think about history in the same way," declared public opinion guru Dan Yankelovich.

Millennials Rising (Vintage, 2000) has been widely quoted in the media for its insistence that today's new crop of teens and kids are very different from Generation X and, on the whole, doing much better than most adults think. "Forget Generation X—and Y, for that matter," says the *Washington Post*, "The authors make short work of most media myths that shape our perceptions of kids these days." According to the *Chronicle of Higher Education*, "Administrators say they can already see indicators of the trends predicted by the authors." "The book is stuffed with interesting nuggets," wrote the *New York Times*. "It is brightly written. And it illuminates changes that really do seem to be taking place." "It's hard to resist the book's hopeful vision for our children and future," added *NEA Today*, "Many of the theories they wrote about in their two previous books—*Generations* and *13th Gen*—have indeed come to pass." In *Millennials and the Pop Culture* (LifeCourse, 2006), the authors apply their generational insights and methodologies to the entertainment industry, and in *Millennials Go to College* (LifeCourse 2007) to academe.

Articles by Howe and Strauss have appeared in the *Harvard Business Review, Atlantic*, the *Washington Post*, the *New York Times, American Demographics, USA Today, USA Weekend*, and other national publications.

Neil Howe is senior associate at the Center for Strategic and International Studies (CSIS) and senior advisor to the Concord Coalition, where he coauthors a quarterly newsletter on the federal budget. Howe has written extensively on budget policy and aging and on attitudes toward economic growth, social progress, and stewardship. He previously coauthored *On Borrowed Time* (1989; reissued 2004), a pioneering call for budgetary reform. He has drafted several Social Security reform plans and testified on entitlements many times before Congress. Howe coauthors numerous publications for the Global Aging Initiative at CSIS, most recently *The Graying of the Great Powers: Demography*

and Geopolitics in the Twenty-First Century. He holds graduate degrees in history and economics from Yale University. He lives in Great Falls, Virginia, with his wife Simona and two children, Giorgia and Nathaniel.

William Strauss's first book, *Chance and Circumstance* (1978) is a widely acclaimed history of the Vietnam draft. Strauss was also a noted playwright, theater director, and performer. He was cofounder and director of the professional satirical troupe Capitol Steps, and performed numerous times with them off-Broadway. Strauss wrote three musicals (*MaKiddo*, *Free-the-Music.com*, and *Anasazi*) and two plays (*Gray Champions* and *The Big Bump*) about themes in the books he coauthored with Howe. In the summer of 1999, he cofounded the Cappies, now an international "Critics and Awards" program for high school students (*www.cappies.com*). In 2006 and 2007, he advised creative teams of high school students who wrote the new musicals *Edit:Undo* (*www.editundo.org*) and *Senioritis* (*www.senioritismusical.com*). Strauss held graduate degrees from Harvard Law School and the Kennedy School of Government. His wife, Janie, serves on the Fairfax County School Board and lives in McLean, Virginia. They have four grown children.

About LifeCourse Associates

LifeCourse Associates is a publishing, speaking, and consulting company built on the generational discoveries of Neil Howe and William Strauss. Using a visionary blend of social science and history, we interpret the qualitative nature of a generation's collective persona to help managers and marketers leverage quantitative data in new and remarkable ways. We offer keynote speeches, seminars, communications products, and consultations that help clients solve marketing and workplace problems and exploit strategic opportunities.

We have served hundreds of clients, including many K–12 school systems, colleges, and federal agencies. Our clients cover a wide range of sectors—from Nike to Merrill Lynch, from Disney to the U.S. Marine Corps, from MTV and Paramount Pictures to the American Petroleum Institute and Ford Motor Company.

To contact LifeCourse Associates
call 866–537–4999
or go to www.lifecourse.com

Sources

Given the vast range of topics covered in this book—and the numberless scholarly, journalistic, and pop culture sources that bear some connection to them—there is no way to reference everything of interest. Readers who wish to dig deeper into the data sources for the behavior and attitude trends described here should consult the comprehensive bibliographic reference section included at the end of *Millennials Rising* (2000). As a convenience, a brief list is provided here of the sources (from publications and websites to programs and agencies) that were of particular use in preparing this book.

Readers who want to find out more about the Strauss-Howe generational perspective on American history are invited to read the authors' previous books: *Generations* (1991), *13th-Gen* (1993), and *The Fourth Turning* (1997). The authors' treatment of the Millennial Generation includes: *Millennials Rising* (2000), *Millennials and the Pop Culture* (2006), *Millennials Go to College* (2nd ed., 2007), and *Millennials in the Workplace* (forthcoming, 2008).

Sources on General Youth Behavior, Summary List

General
The Child and Family Web Guide (Tufts University), website
Child Trends DataBank (Child Trends), website
America's Children (U.S. Federal Interagency Forum on Child and Family Statistics), annual publication
Trends in the Well-Being of America's Children and Youth (U.S. Department of Health and Human Services), 2003
The State of America's Children (Children's Defense Fund), annual publication
The Child and Youth Well-Being Index (Duke University), annual publication

Demographics, Family Structure, Race, Ethnicity, Family Income, Youth Employment
U.S. Bureau of the Census
U.S. Bureau of Labor Statistics (Department of Labor)

Teresa L. Morisi "Youth enrollment and employment during the school
year," *Monthly Labor Review* (Department of Labor)
Teenage Research Unlimited, annual press releases on teen spending

Children's Use of Time

Sandra L. Hofferth and Jack Sandberg, *Changes in American Children's Time, 1981–1997*
(Institute for Social Research and Population Studies Center, University of Michigan), 1998
F. Thomas Juster, Hiromi Ono, Frank P. Stafford, *Changing Times
of American Youth: 1981–2003* (Institute for Social Research and
Population Studies Center, University of Michigan), 2004

Youth Health & Risk Behaviors

U.S. National Center for Health Statistics
Youth Risk Behavior Surveillance System (U.S. Centers for Disease
Control and Prevention), publications and website, 2006
U.S. National Institute of Child Health and Human Development (National
Institutes of Health, Department of Health and Human Services)
Youth Studies Group (Stanford Center for Research in Disease Prevention)

Teen Births, Abortions

U.S. National Center for Health Statistics
Alan Guttmacher Institute, publications and website

Family Dysfunction

U.S. Children's Bureau (Administration on Children, Youth and Families, of the
Administration for Children and Families, Department of Health and Human Services)
U.S. National Center on Child Abuse and Neglect (Administration on
Children, Youth and Families, of the Administration for Children
and Families, Department of Health and Human Services)

Youth Drug Abuse

U.S. Substance Abuse and Mental Health Services Administration (Department
of Health and Human Services), regular publications and website
Lloyd D. Johnston, Jerald G. Bachman, and Patrick M. O'Malley (project direc-
tors), Monitoring the Future Study (Institute for Social Research, University of
Michigan), annual questions to students in grades 12 (since the class of 1975) and
in grades 10 and 8 (since the class of 1991); reports issued in various years
Partnership for a Drug Free America, publications and website

Youth Crime

U.S. National Criminal Justice Reference Service (Department
of Justice), publications and website
National School Safety Center, publications and website

Sources on General Youth Attitudes, Summary List

Drexel Poll

Drexel University Futures Poll: Teenagers, Technology and Tomorrow (Drexel University), 1997

Gallup Polls

Gallup News Service (The Gallup Organization), website

Generation 2001

Generation 2001 Survey (Northwestern Mutual Life), 1999

Youth Marketing

Harris Interactive polls (*Harris Youth Poll*, others in Youth
    Research department), published on website
Ypulse youth marketing website

Horatio Alger

The State of Our Nation's Youth (Horatio Alger Association), annual publication and website

Monitoring the Future

Lloyd D. Johnston, Jerald G. Bachman, and Patrick M. O'Malley (project direc-
    tors), *Monitoring the Future Study* (Institute for Social Research, University of
    Michigan), annual questions to students in grades 12 (since the class of 1975) and
    in grades 10 and 8 (since the class of 1991); reports issued in various years

NASSP

The Mood of American Youth (National Association of Secondary School Principals),
    students aged 13–17 interviewed early in each year; 1974, 1983, and 1996

National Governors Association

Rate Your Future (National Governors Association), 2005

Pew Center

The Pew Research Center for the People and the Press, regular published surveys on youth

Primedia/Roper

The Primedia/Roper National Youth Opinion Survey (Primedia, Inc., Roper Starch
    Worldwide, Inc.), students in grades 7–12 interviewed in Nov. 1998; 1998

Roper Youth Report

Roper Youth Report (Roper Starch Worldwide), annual pub-
    lication, reports issued in various years

UCLA Freshman Poll

L.J. Sax, A.W. Astin, W. S. Korn, and K.M. Mahoney, *The American
    Freshman* (Higher Education Research Institute, University of California
    at Los Angeles), published annually, yearly surveys since 1966

Who's Who

Annual Survey of High Achievers (Who's Who Among American High
    School Students), "high-achieving" high school student inter-
    viewed annually since 1967; published annually and website

YATS

Youth Attitude Tracking Survey (Defense Manpower Data Center, U.S. Department of Defense), survey of potential high school-aged recruits, published annually

Sources on K–12 Student Behavior & Achievement, Summary List

General

The Condition of Education (U.S. National Center for Education Statistics, U.S. Department of Education), annual publication and website
The Digest of Education Statistics (U.S. National Center for Education Statistics), annual publication and website
Terence Deal and Kent Peterson, *Shaping School Culture: The Heart of Leadership*, 2003
David Whitman, *Sweating the Small Stuff: Inner-City School and the New Paternalism*, 2008
Suzanne Lovely and Austin G. Buffum, *Generations at School*, 2007

Academic Achievement

National Assessment of Educational Progress, "The Nation's Report Card" (U.S. Department of Education), regular publications and website
Has Student Achievement Increased Since 2002? State Test Score Trends Through 2006–07 (The Center for Public Education), 2008
Progress in International Reading Literacy Study (International Association), 2006
Trends in International Math and Science Study (International Association), 2007
Rigor at Risk: Reaffirming Quality in the High School Core Curriculum (ACT), 2007
Crisis at the Core: Preparing All Students for College and Work (ACT), 2004
National Curriculum Survey 2005–2006 (ACT), 2006
The College Board, website and publications (e.g., *SAT Reports*), 2008
Raising Our Sights: No High School Senior Left Behind (National Commission on the High School Senior Year), 2001
Getting Serious about High School Graduation Rates (Southern Regional Executive Board), 2005

Attitudes of Students, Teachers, Parents, and Employers

High School Survey of Student Engagement (Indiana University School of Education), annual publication
Life After High School: Young People Talk about Their Hopes and Prospects (Public Agenda), 2005
Voices Study: Research Findings (America's Promise), 2006
The Silent Epidemic: Perspectives of High School Dropouts (Bill & Melinda Gates Foundation), 2006
Cheryl Almeida, Cassius Johnson, and Adria Steinberg, *Making Good on a Promise: What Policymakers Can Do to Support the Educational Persistence of Dropouts* (Jobs for the Future), 2006
A Voice From the Middle: Highlights of the 2007 NASSP/PDK Middle School Student Poll (National Association of Secondary School Principals, Phi Delta Kappa), 2005
Stand by Me (Public Agenda), 2008
Working Without a Net (National Comprehensive Center for Teacher Quality & Public Agenda), 2007
Survey of the American Teacher (MetLife), 2007
Sizing Things Up: What Parents, Teachers, and Students Think About Large and Small High Schools (Public Agenda, Bill & Melinda Gates Foundation), 2002